Royalty

and the

Deeside Railway

W Stewart Wilson
Chris Engel

All profits from this book
will be donated to Alzheimer Scotland
www.alzscot.org

Note: text in *italics* indicates quotations or names

Cover Photos by Jim Henderson

Map of Royal Deeside
Showing route of the Railway

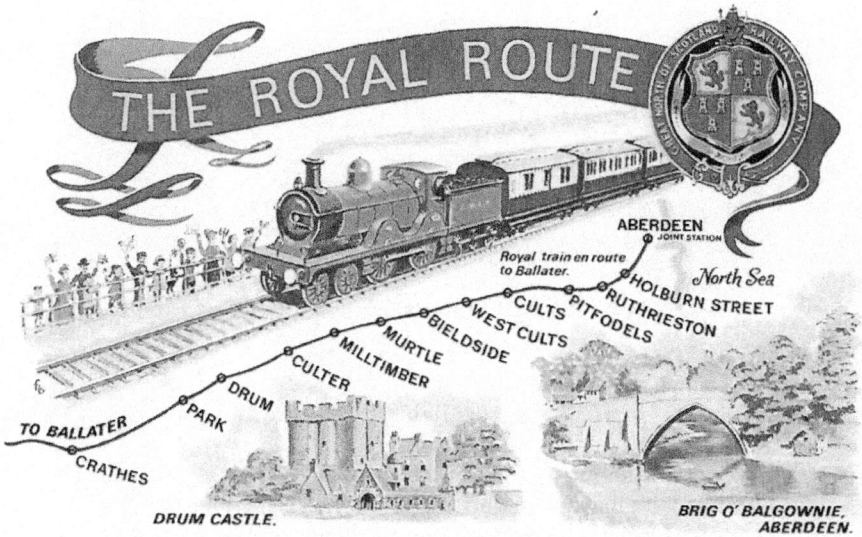

THE ROYAL ROUTE

GREAT NORTH OF SCOTLAND RAILWAY COMPANY

ABERDEEN JOINT STATION

Royal train en route to Ballater.

North Sea

HOLBURN STREET
RUTHRIESTON
PITFODELS
CULTS
WEST CULTS
BIELDSIDE
MURTLE
MILLTIMBER
CULTER
DRUM
PARK
TO BALLATER
CRATHES

DRUM CASTLE.

BRIG O' BALGOWNIE, ABERDEEN.

DELIGHTFUL DEESIDE

GREAT NORTH OF SCOTLAND RAILWAY COMPANY

STRATHDON

BALMORAL CASTLE.

Company's Bus near Ballater.

BY RAIL
& ROAD

LUMPHANAN
DESS
ABOYNE
TORPHINS
GLASSEL
DINNET
CAMBUS O' MAY
BALLATER
BALMORAL
BRAEMAR
BANCHORY
FROM ABERDEEN

Contents

Preface

The three Rs have long been referred to as the basic skills taught in our schools - *reading, riting and rithmetic.* Deeside, too, can be said to have three Rs - **River**, **Royalty** and **Railway**.

The **River** rises from the Wells of Dee and follows a course of over 137 km to the North Sea at Aberdeen. In the book *Description of the East Coast of Scotland* by F Douglas published in 1782, he writes on the abundance of salmon caught on the Dee: *the take is reckoned to afford yearly about seventy last of salmon.* A *last* is an old Scottish measure for twelve barrels with each barrel containing about 113 kg (250 pounds) of fish. That is around 95 tonnes of salmon per year or 24,000 individual fish! The Dee today may no longer be the once plentiful river for salmon but it is just as picturesque. *On its sparkling waters not a single reach of its scenery lacks beauty or interest,* wrote Alex McConnachie in 1893.

Royalty found the pleasures and beauties of the valley well over a thousand years ago. In the eighth century Angus, King of the Picts, built a timber fort near where Braemar castle is today. Over 200 years elapsed before the next royal visitor; King Kenneth II came on a hunting trip and gave his name to the hill overlooking Braemar - *Creag Choinnich* in Gaelic or Craig Kenneth. Kings Malcolm II and Malcolm III were also frequent visitors. It is claimed that in 1064 Malcolm III and his Queen held a gathering and awarded prizes for strength and skill including a race up Creag Choinnich. Today much the same takes place each year at the Braemar Gathering. On Thursday 14 September 1848, Queen Victoria and her family attended the highland games for the first time, held that year at Invercauld House. Since then, members of the royal family have attended almost every year and today the games are attended by thousands of others from all over the world. On Thursday 4 September 1952, the year of accession of our late Queen, there was a record attendance of 31,000 arriving on 437 buses and 2536 cars! It was only in 1968 that the games day changed from being held on a Thursday to the first Saturday in September. Today Braemar's population of around 900 increases to around 20,000 on games day.

The Braemar Gathering, 14 Sep 1848

DEESIDE RAILWAY.

The **Railway**, which opened as far as Banchory in 1853, extended first to Aboyne in 1859 and finally to Ballater in 1866, was instantly popular with the Royal family. It was on Thursday 13 October 1853, just a month after the opening of the line, that Queen Victoria and Prince Albert made the journey along the line from Banchory to Ferryhill at the end of their summer visit. Kings, queens and emperors all travelled the line over the next 113 years until it closed in 1966. The royal family's love for this part of Scotland continues and has allowed the valley to earn the name **Royal Deeside**.

The Building of the Deeside Line

Before the Railway

The turnpike road, replacing the old Deeside road, was completed in three sections; in 1798 from Aberdeen as far as Mills of Drum, by 1802 it had reached Charleston of Aboyne, but it was not until 1855 that the new road reached Braemar. Transport on Deeside was by coach and in the *New Deeside Guide* by author James Brown, published in 1843, we get an idea of the time taken for the journey. *The Mail Coach leaves Aberdeen every morning at seven o'clock - and letters must be put into the Post Office by twenty minutes past six. It reaches Banchory at half-past nine - Kincardine O'Neil at eleven - Charleston of Aboyne about half-past eleven, and Ballater at one.*

Note: It was only in 1869, three years after the death of 'James Brown', that it was discovered that the author was actually Joseph Robertson who had written his first guide in 1831 at the age of 21 while on holiday in Ballater.

The Line to Banchory

It was in 1845 that a board was formed to consider the building of a Deeside railway to improve communications and travel. It was estimated that building a single line along the north bank of the Dee to Banchory would cost £95,000, or £220,000 to reach Aboyne. The proposed line from Banchory would follow the turnpike road through Inchmarlo estate which then stretched from just east of Glassel road at Banchory extending westwards to nearly as far as Potarch. Duncan Davidson was the then owner of the estate and, along with other local landowners, was not happy with the proposed route.

In 1845 the Aberdeen Railway Company had won support to build the railway from Aberdeen to the south which required a bridge to cross the Dee. It was agreed that there should be a delay until its temporary station at Ferryhill was completed.

An Act of Parliament for building of a railway from Ferryhill to Charleston of Aboyne received Royal Assent on 16 July 1846 but there were to be delays.

Railway bridge over the River Dee at Aberdeen and Ferryhill junction 1850

The building of Ferryhill station was completed in early 1850 and on Saturday 30 March the line linking Aberdeen to the south was officially opened. The *Aberdeen Press and Journal* reported that *at 8 o'clock the Directors and a party of ladies made the formal opening trip which was performed in excellent style.*

In the same year negotiations began with local landowners for the building of the first section of the Deeside line.

On 28 May 1852 the Deeside Railway Company obtained Royal Assent for a railway from Aberdeen, terminating at or near the Free Church at Banchory. At that time, the Free Church in Banchory was on the north side of the Aberdeen to Aboyne turnpike immediately west of what is now Raemoir Road. Less than six weeks later, on 5 July 1852, Mrs Kinloch, the wife of Alexander Kinloch of Park House, one of the directors of the Deeside Railway, cut the first turf near the Mains of Drum.

The laying of the line went ahead and the new railway was ready for its first passengers on 7 September 1853.

Cutting the first turf at Drum

But it might not have happened. In the *Edinburgh Advertiser* with the heading *Diabolical Attempt,* it was reported: *At the trial trip of the Deeside Railway last week an attempt was made to throw the train off the rails - one of the lengths of line having been lifted by some miscreant. Fortunately the circumstances were noticed in time to avert the consequences that must otherwise have followed.*

Two hundred invitations were issued for the official opening of the line at Ferryhill Station, Aberdeen. On the arrival of the train at Banchory, the guests were entertained to lunch in the Burnett Arms Hotel during which John Watson, one of the most influential Banchory residents, presented a petition on behalf of the residents that the line be called the Banchory Railway. John Duncan, Chairman of the Deeside Railway, assured him that the petition would be considered. This pleased Watson, but clearly Duncan already had his eye on a possible extension beyond Banchory-Ternan. The following day the service opened to the public with stations at Cults, Murtle, Culter, Park, Mills of Drum, Crathes Castle and Banchory. Initially there were three trains a day, taking about an hour to travel the 27 km. Stations at Milltimber and Drum were provided in the following year and soon after a station was opened at Ruthrieston.

With the opening of the line to Banchory, the proprietors of the Deeside horse-drawn coaches announced the immediate withdrawal of the *Prince of Wales* and the *Marquis of Huntly* coaches between Aberdeen and Banchory but until the railway extended to Ballater, *The Banks of Dee* continued to carry mail to upper Deeside. Charles Cook of the Huntly Arms hotel in Aboyne provided a coach service between Banchory and Aboyne to connect with the trains at Banchory.

In 1863 the private platforms at Crathes Castle, situated at the Milton of Crathes, and the small station at Mills of Drum, were closed and replaced by a new station at Crathes. Ease of transport to Aberdeen by railway was also wanted by those living south of the river and bridges were built to provide access to stations where previously ferries and fords had been the only means of crossing the Dee.

Banchory village in the mid-nineteenth century, soon after the Deeside Line was opened.

Extension to Aboyne

The Huntly Arms Hotel, Aboyne c1870

The line was a financial success and it was suggested that the line from Banchory should continue to Lumphanan and, by way of Cushnie, to Alford. Another scheme, supported by the Deeside Railway Company, suggested that a railway be built from Colford, often written as Coalford, near Culter, which was on the Deeside line, and reach Alford by way of Echt, Waterton and Tillyfourie. Neither scheme gained support from Parliament and in November 1856 plans were announced to extend the line from Banchory to Aboyne. Royal Assent was granted to the Deeside Extension Railway Company on 27 July 1857. The first turf was cut on 2 October that year at Rosehill, near Charleston of Aboyne, by the Marchioness of Huntly, wife of the 10th Marquis. After the open-air proceedings concluded, the three hundred guests walked to a marquee on the Aboyne Green where lunch was served, prepared by Charles Cook and his wife of the Huntly Arms hotel. There had been a coaching inn on the site of the hotel since 1432. In 1848 the 9th Marquis of Huntly had appointed Charles Cook as landlord of the Huntly Arms hotel. He was well qualified for the job of looking after the hotel coaching business, having for many years been a driver of the *Defiance* stage-coach between Aberdeen and Edinburgh, which had been used frequently by the 9th Marquis.

The proposed plan of 1846 had a route passing through Kincardine O' Neil but Patrick Davidson of Inchmarlo made it very clear that he opposed the line passing within sight of his mansion. The survey of 1846 saw the line passing to the south of the village on an embankment and crossing the river about 0.8 km to the west and about 1.6 km further on re-crossing it from south to north above the Mill of Dess. The route would have been both unpopular and expensive. The solution was that the line should leave Banchory and head in a more northerly direction to Lumphanan before returning south to Aboyne. Patrick Davidson, a director of the Deeside Railway Company, sold land east of the Glassel Road in 1858 to allow the railway extension to be built. A newspaper of that year reports that work is progressing well and in particular *the bridge which crosses the turnpike west of Banchory is ready to receive the beams. We may therefore expect, that, by next summer, if the works are carried on with the full complement of men, as at present, to see the line opened for traffic.* A major piece of engineering was the railway viaduct which was designed by John Willet and crossed the Beltie burn west of Torphins. It was not until 2 December 1859 that the first passenger train ran on the extended line to Aboyne with intermediate stations at Glassel, Torphins, Lumphanan and Dess.

The Royal Train crossing the Beltie Viaduct between Torphins and Lumphanan

Aboyne and Braemar Railway Company

It was now inevitable that there would be a proposal for a further extension of the line to reach the whole of Deeside. The extension was proposed by an independent company called the Aboyne and Braemar Railway Company. The proposal was that the line from Aboyne should, after passing through a tunnel, follow the north bank of the Dee to Ballater. From there the route would follow the turnpike and cross by a bridge to the south bank for the last 5 km (3 miles) to Braemar, terminating at a station just short of the Invercauld Arms hotel. There was even the suggestion that the railway could be extended beyond Braemar and join the Highland line at Blair Atholl or that a line be built through Glen Feshie to a junction with the railway at Kingussie.

In 1864 Col James Farquharson, 13th laird of Invercauld estate, located on the opposite bank to Balmoral and closer to Braemar, not only gave his support to the proposal but was appointed chairman of the Aboyne and Braemar Railway Company. The proposed railway would be of benefit to him for transporting timber from his estate, but he thought it wise to consult Queen Victoria as he did not want to risk upsetting her. The Queen was put in an embarrassing situation, wanting to keep in good terms with her neighbour, but at the same time completely opposed to the idea of a railway passing close to Balmoral. She instructed Sir Charles Phipps, Keeper of the Privy Purse to write to Farquharson: *The Queen feels so strongly that she thinks its existence in the neighbourhood of Balmoral would go far to destroy all her enjoyment of the place.* The letter must have caused Col Farquharson to reconsider his position, for at a public meeting held in Ballater in April 1865, attended by a large number of residents from Ballater and Braemar, his factor, William Brown, who chaired the meeting, was extremely diplomatic in what he shared with those present. He said: *You are aware that the Bill, as first brought before the House of Commons, was called The Aboyne and Braemar Railway; but this has been somewhat altered owing to circumstances not easily explainable, opposition of an unreasonable and peculiar nature, little expected, and also in my opinion for want, perhaps, of thorough enthusiasm by its promoters.* This was an early indication that all was not well with the proposal and that it had opposition from Queen Victoria. The meeting agreed to petition Parliament in favour of the railway from Aboyne to Ballater. This found favour with those from Braemar and in thanking the Chairman, their representative said that *if the proper course was taken; they would have a railway to Ballater before eighteen months was over; and when it got the length of Braemar they would give it a push over the hills, and send it into Perthshire.* Obviously, they were not going to concede defeat just yet.

On 11 May a committee at Westminster met to discuss the bill and considered the objections received, which were three in number. One from a Mrs Shepherd of Craigendarroch Cottage whose house would overlook the proposed line, a second from the trustees of Ballater road on engineering matters which had been resolved, and a third in the name of the Marchioness of Huntly which was dismissed when her agent seemed confident that an agreement, although not yet signed, had been reached. The compromise was that the terminus was to be Ballater with a further 2.4 km to Bridge of Gairn to be used solely for goods traffic. A D Farr in his book, *The Royal Deeside Line,* quotes from the minutes of the Deeside Railway Company that on 25 May 1865 it was agreed that the *company was under obligations not at any time hereafter to apply for or promote or in any way directly or indirectly assist in the formation or working of any railway up the valley of the Dee for passenger traffic above the said proposed terminal station at Ballater or for goods traffic above the proposed terminus on the Waterside of the Bridge of Gairn.* The agreement was signed by John Duncan, Chairman of the Deeside Railway Company and Arnold William White, solicitor to Queen Victoria. The Queen had won and there was never an attempt to extend the railway to Braemar during her lifetime. However, in 1919, there was a proposal to build a light railway from Ballater to Braemar as a means of relieving the pressure on the road, but the scheme quickly hit the buffers.

The Bill, as amended, received Royal assent on 5 July 1865 and the ceremony of cutting the first turf was held at Ballater on 7 September 1865 by Mrs Farquharson of Invercauld. To mark the event, the customary dinner was held at the Invercauld Arms hotel attended (among others) by Col James Farquharson, chairman of the new company, and William Brown, factor of Invercauld, and representing the Deeside Railway, John Duncan, chairman, and Sir Alexander Anderson, who had come by train from Aberdeen to Aboyne and then by carriage to Ballater. Less than thirteen months later on 17 October 1866, the first train reached Ballater with an intermediate station at Dinnet. An additional station at Cambus O' May was opened in 1876.

The ground from Ballater to Bridge of Gairn was prepared for a light railway to carry timber from Ballochbuie forest, then owned by Col James Farquharson of Invercauld. the 13th laird. It was to connect with a tramway which he was proposing to construct for about 19 km to Braemar to carry the wood traffic from the Ballochbuie forest. The rails to Bridge of Gairn were actually laid but the tramway was never constructed. Work was suddenly stopped when the forest was leased by Queen Victoria and bought outright by her in 1878 to prevent it being bought for the felling of timber.

Ballochbuie Forest

To mark this significant event, the Queen had a cairn erected on the Balmoral Estate with the inscription:

**QUEEN VICTORIA ENTERED INTO POSSESSION OF THE BALLOCHBUIE 15th MAY 1878.
THE BONNIEST PLAID IN SCOTLAND**

The *Bonniest Plaid in Scotland* recalls the old legend that McGregor, the last laird of Ballochbuie, sold the forest to Farquharson of Invercauld for a tartan plaid.

Preliminary work had also been done in preparation for the erection of a railway bridge over the Gairn just west of Ballater but it was never required. The bridge, although ordered and delivered, it was never erected and instead was built further up the Gairn to provide access to Daldownie, where it can still be seen.

Initially a horse-drawn carriage was provided to take passengers to Braemar, but after the introduction of buses it was left to Great North of Scotland Railway (GNSR) to introduce a quicker transfer. On 2 May 1904 two services on weekdays were introduced connecting with the arrival of trains at Ballater.

The GNSR was the first railway company in Scotland to operate motor coaches. The route was by way of Bridge of Gairn, Abergeldie, Crathie, Inver and Bridge of Dee, arriving at the Invercauld Arms Hotel and Fife Arms Hotel after a journey of about 1½ hours. The Braemar depot was built behind the Invercauld Arms hotel and later was used by the bus company serving Braemar. It has now been converted into housing, complete with a restored *Great North of Scotland Railway* sign on the front elevation. In 2023 a planning application was granted for change of use to offices for the Invercauld Arms and Fife Arms Hotels.

On 1 September 1866 the Deeside Railway Company was leased to the GNSR, and became part of the latter in 1876. In 1864 GNSR had been given powers to construct a railway through the valley of the Denburn to a new station at Aberdeen that became known as the Joint Station. It replaced the station on Waterloo Quay in Aberdeen which had been the terminus of GSNR in the city. The new station was in Guild Street and was a much-needed replacement for the station of 1854, the terminus of both the Deeside Railway and the Aberdeen Railway. The Joint Station was opened in 1867 and was managed by a joint committee of the GNSR and the Caledonian Railway, the latter having absorbed the Scottish North Eastern Railway which in turn had taken over the Aberdeen Railway. In 1923 GNSR became part of the London and North Eastern Railway (LNER) before being absorbed by British Railways in 1948.

Strathspey, Strathdon and Deeside Junction Railway

In 1884 a very ambitious proposal was made by the 11th Marquis of Huntly among others, to connect Strathdon with Deeside. The route would start from a junction east of Nethy Bridge and meet the Deeside line 0.8 km east of Cambus O' May, a distance of 68 km. The promoters considered that such a line would boost tourism. The GNSR was not prepared to support the scheme financially but would be prepared to work the railway when constructed. Parliament however, did not support the scheme, and no more was heard of the project.

A proposal for a new Kincardineshire Railway

Before leaving the development of the Deeside line, near the end of Queen Victoria's reign, there was an interesting proposal for a new line. A public meeting was convened to consider *the furthering of the movement for the construction of a railway which has been occupying the attention of the men of the Mearns and the inhabitants of the Deeside district for some months back*. The meeting was held in October 1898 in Laurencekirk. The proposal was to build a line from Laurencekirk to Aboyne. The route would leave the Caledonian main line at Laurencekirk and join the Deeside branch of the GNSR near Craigwell by Aboyne. The line would go via Auchenblae to Strachan and then follow the south side of the river Dee before crossing the river near Carlogie, reaching Craigwell 1.6 km from Aboyne. It was argued that such a line *would be of the greatest convenience and use to the proprietors, residenters, and farmers in the Feugh and upper Dee valleys, all of whom are practically cut off from the south by want of such communication.*

The saving in distance by this line compared with the present detour by Aberdeen was claimed to be almost 50 km *saving the Queen at least an hour's journey time going to and returning from Balmoral.* Nothing came of the proposal.

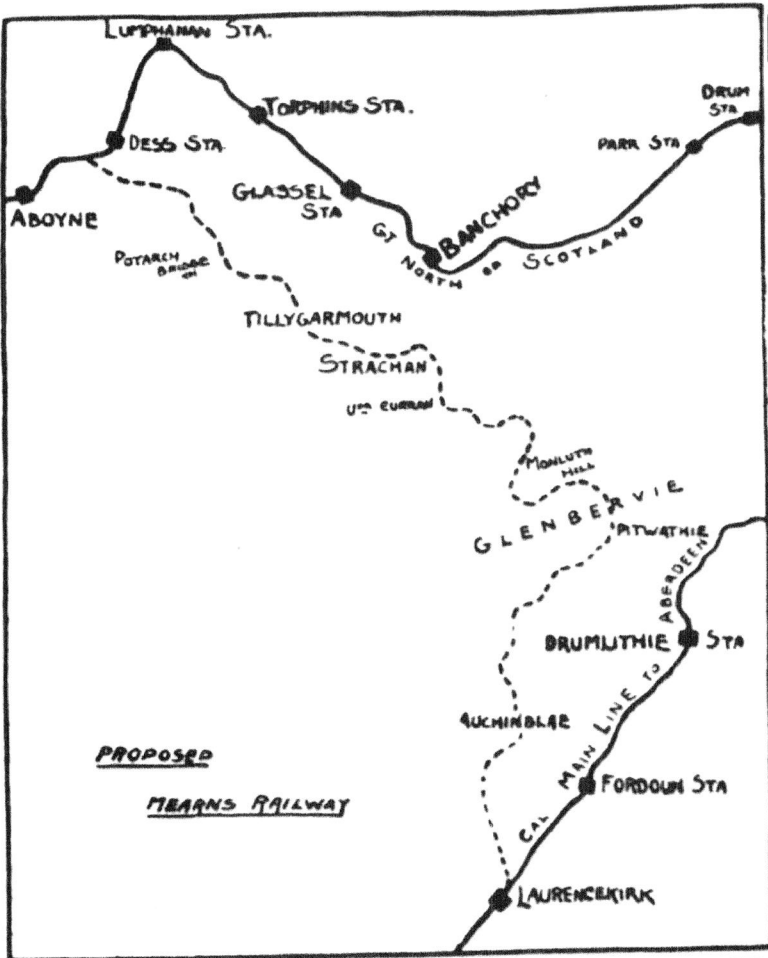

PROPOSED NEW KINCARDINESHIRE RAILWAY.

LAURENCEKIRK TO ABOYNE.

DETAILS OF SCHEME–SKETCH OF ROUTE.

Victoria and Albert

The visit of George IV to Scotland in 1822 was the first visit of a reigning British monarch to Scotland for nearly two centuries. The previous visit was by King Charles II for his Scottish coronation at Scone on 1 January 1651, which was New Year's Day in Scotland, whereas in England it was still the year 1650. It was not until 1752 that the date for the start of the year changed from 25 March to 1 January in England, whereas in Scotland, this was done in 1600, during the reign of James VI.

The Deeside Railway between Aberdeen and Banchory opened in 1853 and quickly became very popular with tourists. It was also well-used by Queen Victoria and Prince Albert. The story of how the Queen became so in love with this part of Scotland is fascinating.

Victoria becomes Queen

Princess Alexandrina Victoria of Kent came to the throne a month after her eighteenth birthday on 20 June 1837. When she was born on 24 May 1819, she was fifth in line to succession after the four sons of George III. When he died in 1820, he was succeeded first by his eldest son who became George IV. The new king had no surviving children and so next in line would have been Frederick Duke of York - but he died in 1827. When George IV died in 1830, the throne passed to the next surviving brother, William, Duke of Clarence thus becoming William IV. He too had no surviving family to follow him on the throne. The youngest of the four brothers was Edward, Duke of Kent (who died in 1820); hence his daughter Victoria became heir presumptive after the death of her uncle William IV.

Victoria's mother, the Duchess of Kent, had two brothers, Leopold, who had become King of Belgium in 1831, and Ernest II, Duke of Saxe-Coburg and Gotha. It was Leopold who suggested that the Duchess of Kent should invite the Duke of Saxe-Coburg and Gotha and his son Albert to visit her in May 1836, with the purpose of meeting Victoria. After the visit, Victoria wrote to her uncle Leopold to thank him *for the prospect of great happiness you have contributed to give me, in the person of dear Albert.* Albert made another visit along with his father in October 1839 to visit the Queen, with the objective of a proposal of marriage. The couple were married on 10 February 1840.

Queen Victoria's Coronation, 28 June 1838.
(Royal Collection Trust / © His Majesty King Charles III 2024)

Queen Victoria and Prince Albert's wedding, 10th February 1840
(Royal Collection Trust / © His Majesty King Charles III 2024)

Her First Train Journey

It was on 13 June 1842 that Queen Victoria first travelled by train. She, with Prince Albert and some of the family, left Windsor that day for the short journey from Slough to Paddington station in London. It was thought advisable that the royal children should not accompany them on the train and they were taken by road to Buckingham Palace. The specially adapted royal carriage for the Queen and Prince Albert was placed in the middle of the train and suitably decorated for the occasion. We are told that the engine was driven by Daniel Gooch, the railway's superintendent locomotive engineer, accompanied on the footplate by Isambard Kingdom Brunel, the great engineer and builder of the Great Western Railway. Brunel had built the Great Western Railway to his unique broad gauge of 2.1m (7 feet) between the rails as he thought this would give extra speed and comfort. The journey had only taken 25 minutes at a speed of 48 km/h (30 mph). The following day Victoria wrote in her diary:

We arrived here yesterday morning (Buckingham Palace)*, having come by the railroad, from Windsor, in half an hour, free from dust and crowd and heat, and I am quite charmed with it.*

Such was her first favourable impression of rail travel that, when a month later, they made the return journey to Windsor, the Princess Royal and the eight-month-old Prince of Wales accompanied them. That was to be the first of many journeys by rail for Queen Victoria's children and many of these were later to be on the Deeside line.

In 2017 to mark the 175th the anniversary of Victoria's first train journey, Her Late Majesty Queen Elizabeth II recreated same journey, covering the distance in 10 minutes. They were joined by Isambard Thomas, Brunel's great-great-great-grandson, who sat next to the Queen. Sitting opposite was Gillian White, the great-great-granddaughter of Sir Daniel Gooch, who drove the original train.

Queen Victoria and family arrive at Slough station.

The first Royal carriage

Early Visits to Scotland

Queen Victoria and Prince Albert first visited Scotland in 1842. They left Windsor early on Monday 29 August and travelled by train to London and on to Woolwich where they joined the *Royal George* yacht. At that time, it was not possible to travel to Scotland by rail. They were thankful when they reached Leith on Thursday 1 September after what had been a somewhat rough voyage. During this first visit they stayed in Edinburgh and at Taymouth Castle in Perthshire, the home of the Marquess of Breadalbane.

Royal Yacht, the Royal George
(Royal Collection Trust / © His Majesty King Charles III 2024)

They returned to Scotland on 9 September 1844 and once again the journey was by sea. This time the weather was kind for the passage to Dundee aboard the new royal yacht *Victoria and Albert,* which had been launched in April 1843.

Royal Yacht the Victoria and Albert I
(Royal Collection Trust / © His Majesty King Charles III 2024)

They stayed at Blair Castle as guests of Lord and Lady Glenlyon, who had given up their home for the Queen's visit. The countryside much impressed the Queen, who wrote on Thursday 8 October during the return voyage: *I was so attached to the dear, dear Highlands, and miss the fine hills so much. There was great peculiarity about the Highlands and Highlanders, and they are chivalrous, fine, active people. Our stay among them was so delightful.* This no doubt prompted the Queen to return to Scotland three years later, but this time the visit was not blessed with good weather.

The royal yacht *Victoria and Albert* left on 11 August 1847 and the royal party were able to enjoy *a delightful voyage and tour among the Western Lochs and Isles - they are so beautiful, and so full of poetry and romance, traditions, and historical associations,* the Queen wrote in her diary on reaching Ardverikie on Loch Laggan on 20 August.

It was to be their holiday home for a month. The weather was far from kind and the Queen's doctor, Sir James Clark, who had travelled with them, persuaded them to try the drier climate of Deeside and suggested Balmoral. He did so on the recommendation of his son, John, who had stayed that summer as a guest of Sir Robert Gordon, his chief in the diplomatic service. During this holiday he had written regularly to his father describing the glorious sunshine and the beauties of Deeside.

In early times the lands of Balmoral formed part of the earldom of Mar. The original castle was built in the fifteenth century and consisted of a square tower with battlements. By 1746 a house had been added to it by the Farquharsons of Inverey. When Sir Robert Gordon, a younger brother of the 4th Earl of Aberdeen, acquired the lease in 1830, he demolished most of the building. He employed John Smith, Aberdeen city architect, to design a small castle in a mixture of Tudor and Scottish Baronial style. Sir Robert died suddenly in October 1847, whereupon his lease on Balmoral reverted to his brother. In February 1848 Prince Albert acquired the remaining part of it, without having seen the property!

Balmoral Castle 1848

Old Balmoral – Their Highland Home

Arrival at Aberdeen 1848

The Queen arrived with her family at Aberdeen on Friday 8 September 1848 aboard the royal yacht, *Victoria and Albert,* and as she travelled up the Deeside road to view the Balmoral estate for the first time, her carriage passed under twenty three triumphal arches.

Triumphal arch at Crathes

She quickly absorbed the spirit of relaxation in the Highland environment and as she remarked at the time - *all seemed to breathe freedom and peace and to make us forget the world and its turmoils.*

Thus began the royal association with Deeside which continues to this day.

Halt at the Burnett Arms Inn at Banchory 1848

The journey was repeated the following August when the Queen travelled to Scotland once again aboard the royal yacht, first calling at Cork, Dublin and Belfast on the Queen's first visit to Ireland. After disembarking at Glasgow the royal party travelled by rail to Perth and then by coach to Spittal of Glenshee and Castleton of Braemar, arriving at Balmoral on 15 August.

The planned return journey was by sea on 28 September, but the weather forecast was not good and it was decided that their return should be by land. Accordingly, on the morning of the following day, the Queen and her family left by coach to Aberdeen and along the turnpike road to the nearest railway point, Montrose station, of the yet unfinished Aberdeen line.

The summer holiday at Balmoral was now well established and in 1851 Her Majesty, after leaving Holyrood Palace in Edinburgh on Friday 29 August, travelled by train to Stonehaven. The new route was chosen to save the Queen the inconvenience of travelling over the inferior roads from Coupar Angus to Balmoral.

Victoria arrives at Perth, August 1849

Four carriages had been sent by sea from London to Aberdeen for Her Majesty and her family. David Robertson, owner of the Royal Hotel in Aberdeen, was tasked that the carriages be taken to Stonehaven. On the morning of 20 August, sixteen horses drawing these carriages and eight other horses were sent by him to await the arrival of the Queen.

The journey was not without incident. At one of the tolls, on the turnpike road, Alexander Gray, the tacksman, demanded that the toll be paid. Robertson claimed that as they were royal carriages, they were exempt and complained to the trustees of the turnpike and lodged a legal appeal. Robertson lost his appeal before the Sherriff of Kincardineshire who ruled that at the time, the carriages were not being used for the conveyance of Her Majesty.

Queen Victoria departing for Balmoral from Stonehaven Station

The Queen and her family arrived at one o'clock and had lunch in a room at the station before travelling to Balmoral in an open carriage, accompanied by Prince Albert, the Prince of Wales and the Princess Royal. A newspaper report of the time recorded that *the wind blew keenly across the mountains, but the royal party encountered it without hesitation; the other royal children followed in a closed carriage alone. Lord John Russell (her Prime Minister at the time), Sir James Clark, Colonel Gordon, and others had no better means of conveyance than an inconvenient char-a-banc. The Premier took the front place, and prepared for a drive of five hours in the teeth of the blast. Banchory formed the terminus of the first stage - a long 15 miles. The cortege wound along by the Dee, which presents endless variety of scenery, through Kincardine, Charleston, Aboyne to Ballater, where it crosses over to the south bank. At half-past six o'clock the Queen and royal party arrived at Balmoral.*

At the end of the holiday on the 7 October the same route was followed in reverse and the royal party joined the train at Stonehaven for a visit to the County of Lancaster.

Old Balmoral Castle, October 1853
(Royal Collection Trust / © His Majesty King Charles III 2024)

In June 1852 the old castle and estate of Balmoral was purchased by Prince Albert for a cost of £31,500 from the trustees of the Earl of Fife. Soon after, the Queen received a £500,000 bequest in the will of the wealthy and eccentric John Camden Nield. In her diary for 1852 the Queen records *a very handsome fortune had inexplicably been bequeathed to me.* This no doubt contributed to the decision to demolish the old castle and use the bequest to build the new Balmoral in its place. Prince Albert summoned William Smith, City Architect of Aberdeen, to visit him at Balmoral on 8 September 1852 and asked him to prepare plans for a new castle, as the current one was considered not large enough for the royal family. Smith suggested a new site 100 yards north-west from the original one, considered to have a better vista.

When the plans were submitted for Prince Albert's approval, he paid close attention to the detail and suggested that amendments be made to the turrets and windows. The foundation stone was laid by Queen Victoria on 28 September 1853, with William Smith in attendance, having travelled by train on the newly opened Deeside line to Banchory and then by carriage to Balmoral. Queen Victoria in her diary detailed the arrangements for the laying of the foundation stone: *The trowel will then be delivered to Her Majesty by Mr Smith of Aberdeen, the architect, and the mortar having been spread, the stone will be lowered.*

The Royal Line opens to Banchory

The first royal to use the Deeside line was the Duchess of Kent, Queen Victoria's mother, who travelled from Banchory to Aberdeen on Tuesday 11 October 1853, followed two days later by the Queen and Prince Albert. When the Deeside Railway Company heard that the Queen was planning to make the journey south, and knowing that the station was not yet complete, arrangements were made to make the stationmaster's house, situated on the corner of what is now Station Road and Glebe Park, available for the Queen to use before boarding her train. Gordon Walkden, in his book, *About Banchory* suggests that the house was *freshly painted, wall papered and had a red carpet laid in anticipation of the Queen requiring lunch.* After two changes of horses and with the weather far from favourable, the Queen's carriage arrived 25 minutes behind schedule. After being greeted by Mr William Innes of Raemoir, Convener of the County of Kincardine, the Queen and Prince Albert joined the train immediately, but not before she suggested that she *desired to have luncheon at Banchory station the following year.* The Queen commented on the journey to Aberdeen: *At Banchory we got into the train, going by a line which is quite new and has only been open for a few weeks. It passes close to Aberdeen and is a great improvement.*

On reaching Ferryhill, Sir Thomas Blaikie, Provost of Aberdeen, and the other dignitaries met the royal party to bid them farewell to Deeside and promised them a warm welcome again. Guild Street Station in Aberdeen was opened in August 1854. Ferryhill Junction was then closed for passenger traffic but was much the preferred as the junction for royal trains during Victoria's reign.

Banchory Railway Station with refreshment room on the left.

On Friday 15 September 1854, Queen Victoria returned, and a newspaper of the day gave a full account of her arrival. By this time the station at Banchory was complete with a wooden refreshment room alongside:

About five minutes past two o'clock the royal party reached Ferryhill, the junction of the Aberdeen and Deeside Railways, and the Directors of the Deeside line having joined the train, it immediately started, the stay at Ferryhill only occupied five or six minutes.

At and around Banchory station were marked by the liveliest signs of welcome and rejoicing, the most conspicuous by far being a magnificent triumphal arch, composed of evergreens, tastefully intermingled with streamers and festoons, the whole being surmounted by handsome crown of flowers. Some idea of the imposing appearance of the structure may be inferred from the fact, that it was no less than between forty and fifty feet in height. From the landing place at the station, to the refreshment rooms where lunch was served, a path of crimson cloth was laid for her Majesty. At exactly forty-five minutes past two, the royal train arrived at

Banchory. On alighting from the carriage, her Majesty, leaning on the arm of the Prince, walked to the refreshment rooms, where luncheon was served in a very elegant style by Mr Grant, of the Burnett Arms Inn. The whole of the royal party appeared to be in excellent spirits, and cordially acknowledged the salutations of the large mass of spectators. At ten minutes past three, the royal party departed, amid the cheers of the crowd, for Balmoral.

Queen Victoria and her family enjoyed almost a month at Balmoral and left shortly after nine o' clock on Thursday 12 October. A full account of the train journey south was contained in the *Aberdeen Journal:*

To Banchory from Balmoral the posting arrangements were under the superintendence of Mr Ross, Ballater and Mr Robertson of the Royal Hotel (Aberdeen) *who performed their duty with their wonted expedition and care, Banchory terminus being reached five minutes by twelve o'clock, twenty minutes earlier than anticipated. At Banchory, John Duncan, Esq., Advocate, Chairman; Patrick Davidson, Esq., of Inchmarlo; A B White, Esq.; and William Henderson, Esq.; Directors of the Deeside Railway were in waiting and conducted the royal party to the railway carriages. The Queen, Prince Albert, the Prince of Wales and the Princess Royal occupied the State Saloon, and the younger branches of the royal family were accommodated in the carriage immediately following that of her Majesty. Lord Aberdeen, Sir James Clark &c, were in the carriages immediately preceding her Majesty. The day continued exceedingly fine. After a delay of almost twenty minutes, the train moved off, amid the hearty cheers of the spectators, at 15 minutes past twelve o' clock. Mr Middleton, stationmaster, had his splendid arch tastefully re-decorated for the occasion.*

When the train approached the Ferryhill junction some 30 minutes later, it was welcomed by a guard of honour and the Directors of the Aberdeen Railway. Another engine was attached to the carriages and preceded by a pilot engine, the train left for the south with a stop at Stonehaven where *the little station was converted into something as like a miniature palace* and lunch was served, *prepared as usual by Mr Douglas of the Douglas hotel.*

The Duchess of Kent and the Royal Line

Abergeldie Castle
(Royal Collection Trust / © His Majesty King Charles III 2024)

Victoria, Duchess of Kent and
mother of Queen Victoria
(Royal Collection Trust
© His Majesty King Charles III 2024)

The estate of Abergeldie was leased in 1848 by Prince Albert and considerable additions were made to make it more comfortable for the reception of guests. It was frequently occupied by the Queen's mother, Duchess of Kent, until her death in 1861. She had been the first royal to use the Deeside line when she travelled from Banchory on Tuesday 11 October 1853.

It is known that on some occasions she rested at the Burnett Arms after leaving the train at Banchory, or at the end of her stay at Abergeldie.

There are press reports that she had lunch there on 8 October 1851 and again on 13 August 1852. This was to continue after the arrival of the railway to Banchory in September 1853 and right up to when it was extended to Aboyne in 1859. It is recorded that she lunched there on 21 August 1855, 15 October 1856, 12 August 1857 and 1 October 1858.

On 10 September 1858 the hotel hosted another royal when the Prince of Wales (later to become Edward VII) had lunch.

BURNETT ARMS' INN, UPPER BANCHORY.

ALEXANDER SIMPSON, late Waiter at the Royal Hotel, Aberdeen, begs to intimate to the Nobility, Commercial Gentlemen, and Public, that he has taken a lease of those new and excellent Premises, at the west end of the Village, which have just now been Painted and Papered in an elegant manner; and hopes to have the Furnishing completed, so as to be open to the Public by the first of May.

A. S. is determined that no expence shall be spared in rendering the House one of the most complete and comfortable on the banks of the Dee, both as regards the furnishing and the selection of Wines and Liquors, &c.

☞ Neat Post Chaises Hearses, and Gigs, with careful Drivers. Also, Saddle Horses. The Mail passes to and from Aberdeen every forenoon.

The "Banks of Dee" Coach was inserted in *Herald* of last week by mistake.

Banchory, 13th April, 1839.

The hotel, dating from 1839, was once a coaching inn.

In the past, the coat-of-arms above the door of the Burnett Arms have been a bit of a mystery. They are most certainly not the arms of the Burnett of Leys family. A letter dated 31 August 1970 from the Court of the Lord Lyon states that *there is no doubt they are the arms of William IV and his spouse Princess Adelaide.*

In an article published in *Leopard Magazine* in September 2000 Gordon Casely, an expert on heraldry, disagrees and claims that the arms are those of the Duchess of Kent, Queen Victoria's mother.

The Burnett Arms on Banchory High Street.
Note the coat-of-arms above the door.

In the article it is stated that HRH the Duchess of Kent (1786 – 1861) was born Victoria, daughter of Francis, Duke of Saxe-Coburg-Saalfeld. She married Edward, Duke of Kent, fourth son of King George III, and their daughter Victoria became Queen in 1837.

The coat of arms above the door

The heraldry of Princess Victoria's marriage shows, on the left, the shield of her husband Edward and on the right, the arms of Saxe-Coburg-Saalfeld through her father. Hence it would seem more appropriate that the arms are those of Queen Victoria's parents rather than the arms of William IV and his spouse Princess Adelaide.

Similar coats of arms can be seen above the entrance to the former Royal Sussex and Victoria Hotel in the Pantiles in Royal Tunbridge Wells and on the Rose and Crown Inn at Tonbridge in Kent.

The Duchess of Kent was generous with granting patronage.

The New Balmoral Castle

In 1854 Prince Albert commissioned George Washington Wilson of Aberdeen, a pioneer of photography, to record progress on the building of the castle and to be paid three guineas a day. Robert Smith in his book *Valley of the Dee* records that *when Washington Wilson left Aberdeen and was whirled away past Dr Morrison's bridge and suburban Cults his equipment was in the luggage van - camera, tent, baskets of chemicals, plate-boxes etc.* George Washington Wilson was to return many times to the castle to take photographs of the family and in 1873 Queen Victoria appointed him Photographer Royal.

William Smith the architect, and Washington Wilson the photographer, kept a watchful eye on the building of the castle and when the Queen arrived at Balmoral on 7 September 1855 she was able to view the almost completed castle but without the tower. It was a memorable visit - three days later came news of the fall of Sevastopol which brought to an end the Crimean War. At that date the railway did not go beyond Banchory and realising the importance of the news, David Middleton, the stationmaster, hired a horse and rode to the castle arriving there between 10pm and 11pm to deliver it.

The new Balmoral castle under construction
(Royal Collection Trust / © His Majesty King Charles III 2024)

A contemporary account reads *all Crathie was soon awake and a huge bonfire was quickly set ablaze on the top of Craig Gowan overlooking the castle, and foregathering around it the foresters, ghillies, attendants and workmen struck up the Queen's Anthem. Her Majesty, Prince Albert, and the royal family assembled at the main entrance to the castle and listened while the loyal strain proceeded. The night was pitch-dark. Silence, save for the rejoicings, prevailed over lofty Lochnagar and his glorious range of neighbours; the Dee soughed along; music from voice and pipe arose; torches, will-o'-the-wisp-like, flashed forth, here, there, everywhere, and the Highland glen scene was one to be remembered. The Queen was greatly pleased with the part Mr Middleton played in the matter, and along with a letter of thanks sent him a cheque for £50.*

The new Balmoral castle after completion

Four days later the Queen and Prince Albert were joined at the castle by Prince Frederick of Prussia who had come by train to ask for the hand of their eldest daughter Princess Victoria.

Queen Victoria and Prince Albert were both very accomplished pianists and singers. Prince Albert was also a keen composer from an early age, and it was their shared love of music that first helped them form an attraction for each other. No wonder then, that on 10 March 1849, John Marr of Aberdeen was granted *Royal Letters Patent by Special Appointment as Pianoforte Maker to Queen Victoria*. Each year, in these early days, he would make the journey to the castle, first to Banchory and then by coach to *run over,* as he himself described, the pianos. He used to recall how the Prince Consort would gather the royal children to his side to watch him at his work *thus affording them some practical insight about the construction of the instrument*. He was highly successful in business and built the beautifully situated Cliff House in Cults. He accepted jokes in good spirit about the name of the house when some of his friends referred to it as *Clef House* while others called it *Piano Fort.*

It was not until the 30 August 1856 that the Queen was able to write in her diary: *On arriving at Balmoral at seven o' clock in the evening we found the tower finished and the poor old house gone! Every year my heart becomes more fixed in this dear Paradise, and so much more so now, that all has become my dear Albert's own creation, own work, own building, own laying out; and his great taste, and the impress of his dear hand, has been stamped everywhere.*

Balmoral Castle viewed from the north-west
(Royal Collection Trust / © His Majesty King Charles III 2024)

On the death of Queen Victoria in 1901, the castle and estate passed, by the terms of her will, to Edward VII and succeeding British monarchs. Today it is a private home of the monarch.

Alex Inkson McConnachie in his book *Deeside* published in 1893, remarked: *before the construction of the Deeside Railway the beauties of the valley were little known, and at the opening few believed the line would prove remunerative.* The railway opened up the area to tourists intrigued by the royal association. The royal family's love for this part of Scotland continues and has allowed the valley to earn the name Royal Deeside.

Florence Nightingale at Birkhall

The Gordons of Abergeldie acquired the estate of Birkhall from the Farquharson family in the year 1715 and built the house. In 1849 Prince Albert purchased it for his son Edward, Prince of Wales, so that he could have a home away from Balmoral. In fact, he only stayed there on one occasion in 1861 much preferring Abergeldie Castle.

In November 1854 Florence Nightingale, along with some nurses, arrived at Scutari in Turkey to tend to the sick and injured soldiers of the Crimean War. Her work was hindered by the dreadful sanitary conditions but the care and attention she paid to the sick - often caring for them late into the night - earned her the name the *Lady of the Lamp*. Queen Victoria admired the work done by Florence Nightingale to improve nursing during the Crimean War, noting in her journal: *I envy her being able to do so much good and look after the noble heroes whose behaviour is admirable.* She also supported Nightingale in practical ways, sending her cases of medical supplies.

In 1856 she sent Florence Nightingale a brooch to honour her service to the military and in the letter she wrote: *It will be a very great satisfaction to me, when you return at last to these shores, to make the acquaintance of one who has set so bright an example to our sex.* The brooch, sometimes called the *Nightingale Jewel*, is thought to have been designed by Prince Albert, and is engraved with a

The Nightingale Jewel
(Royal Collection Trust
© His Majesty King Charles III 2024)

message from the Queen. *To Miss Florence Nightingale, as a mark of esteem and gratitude for her devotion towards the Queen's brave soldiers, from Victoria R.*

After the war, Victoria invited Florence Nightingale to Balmoral. On 19 September 1856 she left Edinburgh where she had been inspecting barracks and hospitals as part of her campaign to set up a Royal Commission to see reform of the Army medical services. She travelled by train to Aberdeen and then to Banchory where she was met and taken by carriage to Birkhall where she was the guest of Sir James Clark, the Queen's physician, who had rented the house. She was accompanied by her father who stayed with her for a few days before returning home.

Florence Nightingale had been to Birkhall in September 1852 to see her sister who was suffering from a medical breakdown and was being cared for by Sir James Clark, a family friend. She had met the Queen informally while out walking but on this visit it was to be very different. On 21 September 1856 she was received by the Queen and Prince Albert at Balmoral and spent an hour with them. Prince Albert wrote: *She put before us all the defects of our present military hospital system, and the reforms that are needed.*

Queen Victoria was most impressed with Florence Nightingale and invited her to attend the ball on the following night marking the opening of the castle's newly completed ballroom. A few days later the Queen came to Birkhall to have tea with her under the lime tree in the garden and asked that she should remain at Birkhall to meet Lord Panmure, Secretary of State for War. He was summoned to Birkhall by the Queen and he had long talks with Florence who convinced him of the need for the setting up of an Army Medical School and the appointment of a Royal Commission.

Florence Nightingale
(Royal Collection Trust
© His Majesty King Charles III 2024)

43

During her stay at Birkhall, Florence received invitations to attend dinners at the castle with the Queen's other guests and on one occasion spent the night at the castle. She left, possibly by train, from Banchory on 9 October, well pleased with the reception she had received from her Queen.

Birkhall in Glen Muick
(Royal Collection Trust / © His Majesty King Charles III 2024)

How appropriate it was that Prince Charles, Duke of Rothesay, now King Charles III, should open the Nightingale hospital in London via a video link from his Scottish home, Birkhall, on Friday 3 April 2020. The hospital had been set up to provide extra beds, if required, to deal with the covid pandemic which was sweeping the country.

The Prince said: *I need hardly say that the name of this hospital could not have been more aptly chosen. Florence Nightingale, The Lady with the Lamp, brought hope and healing to thousands in their darkest hour. In this dark time, this place will be a shining light.*

Brunel Bridge at Balmoral

The old main road through Deeside ran along the south side of the river between Ballater and Braemar, with the Old Bridge of Dee connecting to the military road which crossed from the north bank. However, the road ran very close to the Queen Victoria's Balmoral Castle and concerned about her privacy she, or perhaps more precisely, her Government, approved the new Turnpike Act in 1855 which saw a new road built along the north bank of the river. A bridge was required to link with the north Deeside road. Prince Albert turned his attention to the project and invited Isambard Kingdom Brunel to Balmoral seeking his advice. He admired the engineering genius of Isambard Kingdom Brunel and had met him in 1842 on Queen Victoria's first railway journey from Slough to Paddington when Brunel was on the footplate. Albert had launched Brunel's ship the *Great Britain* in 1843, and he had further dealings with the engineer on the organising committee for the Great Exhibition of 1851. In the autumn of 1854, Prince Albert invited Brunel and his wife Mary to Balmoral. He recommended a possible site for the bridge and made a few sketches before returning to Aberdeen and his train journey south. He later remarked, *didn't have time to stay with Queen Victoria.* In his report to Prince Albert, he said that his plan for the bridge was *the cheapest and most easily erected bridge and if the appearance is considered not objectionable, I should strongly recommend it.* Although he was heavily involved in various other projects it was a contract he could hardly refuse and with the design accepted by Prince Albert, Brunel recommended that it be built by Rowland Brotherhood of Chippenham at a cost of £1650. In May 1855 Brunel wrote to Phipps, Keeper of the Privy Purse: *Brotherhood whose tender is the lowest is a very respectable man. He does a great deal of work of this description for railways and has always given me satisfaction. I understand from him that he is anxious to extend his business northwards and he is therefore likely to do it well.*

Brotherhood was awarded the contract and he immediately started on the work of constructing the iron girders for the bridge, leaving responsibility for the oversight of the building of the of the abutments and approaches to Dr Andrew Robertson.

In 1821 Andrew Robertson had become the sole doctor in the whole of the area and lived at Bridgend, Crathie. Five years later he delivered a baby at Crathienaird. That baby was none other than John Brown. Little did he imagine what the future was to hold for this little boy. In the early 1830s Andrew moved, first to Blelack, and then to Indego on the Cromar estate of the 4th Earl of Aberdeen. The Earl held the lease of Balmoral and knowing of the impending visit by Queen Victoria he approached Robertson and asked him to assist

Dr Andrew Robertson
(Royal Collection Trust
© His Majesty King Charles III 2024)

the royal family on their first visit in 1848. He made a favourable impression and was immediately appointed Commissioner of Queen Victoria's estates on Deeside, a post he held for almost thirty years. In 1851 Robertson gave up his medical practice but continued to act as doctor to members of the royal household at Balmoral. He managed many of the improvements to the estate including the construction of the new Balmoral Castle which was completed in 1855, the Brunel Bridge and the erection of the new Glas-allt-Shiel retreat for the Queen on the shores of Loch Muick. The monarch said of him, *He is highly esteemed, and is a most amiable man, who has carried out all the Prince's and my wishes.*

Angus Buchannan in his book *Brunel, The Life and Times of Isambard Kingdom Brunel* published in 2006, records the frustration of Brunel with Robertson on the building of the bridge. In a letter to him in April 1856 Brunel asked: *Are the piers finished yet for the Balmoral Bridge? The bridge has of course been long finished and is becoming an inconvenience to the manufacturer.*

In September Brunel communicated his annoyance to Phipps on the slow progress of the work locally: *The iron work of the Dee bridge has been completed and tested some nine or ten months since but there does not appear from Dr Robertson's account any prospect of the abutments and approaches being sufficiently advanced to receive it until after the winter. The contractor is in consequence long in arrears of his payments besides having to give a large space in his premises to the bridge. He has pressed me to procure payment on account and I think that £1000 at least should be advanced to him in the usual manner in such cases, on account of work executed.*

Brunel's bridge which crosses the River Dee and links Balmoral
with Crathie on the north.
(Royal Collection Trust / © His Majesty King Charles III 2024)

The Royal Archives has the letter from Brunel on which Phipps marked, *will send him £1000. The bridge may come in November. He had better provide carriage and workmen to put it up. Answered September 12.* Brunel, on receiving a reply from Phipps pointing out *I am most afraid it is too late in the season for him to commence. I have written to him however to proceed, if he possibly can.* Brotherhood immediately organised that the girders be transported in sections by rail to Banchory on the Deeside railway and then by road to Balmoral.

But there were further delays and the bridge was not completed until the autumn of 1857 by which time there were clear signs of the displeasure of the royal family, especially the Queen, with the simplicity of the design. This was communicated by Phipps to

Brunel who was clearly upset and replied: *I am much disappointed at your report of the appearance of the bridge at Balmoral. I confess I had hoped for a very different result and thought at all events the perfect simplicity of the construction and absence of any attempt at ornament would secure it from being in any way unsightly or offensive which I think is always a great first step, but I fear your expression of not extremely ornamental implies something very much the reverse. As regards the elasticity I trust that it is not felt to any extent that is unpleasant as it is unavoidable. But with regard both to the appearance and the stiffness, I will take an early opportunity of seeing it myself.* Whether Brunel did visit Balmoral to view the completed bridge is not known.

As well as Queen Victoria expressing her displeasure, this seems to have been shared by others. G M Fraser in his book *The Old Deeside Road* says little about this bridge and even Fenton Wyness in his book *Royal Valley* fails to mention Brunel. Brunel was proud of his design and described it as a fine example of *functional elegance.* In 2002, in a BBC poll, he took second place to Churchill as the greatest Briton. The Balmoral bridge is his only legacy in Scotland but it took until 2006 before the late Duke of Edinburgh unveiled a plaque, which for the first time makes mention of its designer.

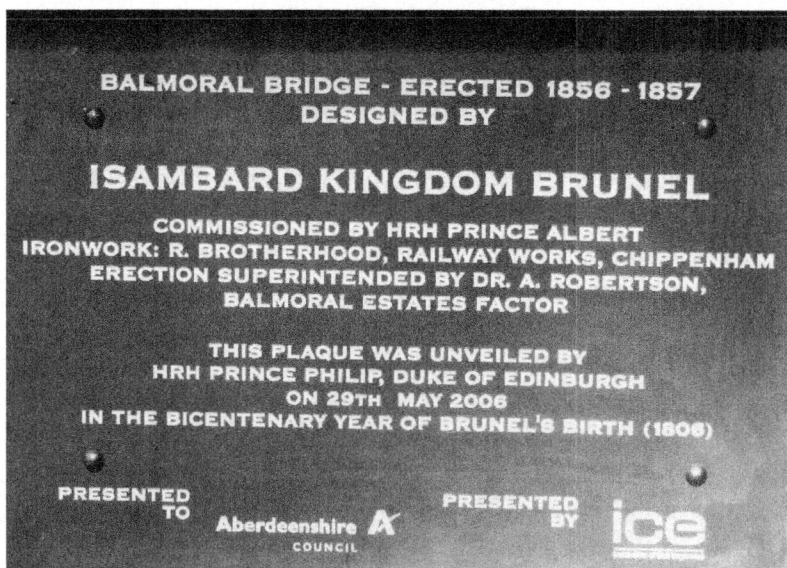

BALMORAL BRIDGE - ERECTED 1856 - 1857
DESIGNED BY

ISAMBARD KINGDOM BRUNEL

COMMISSIONED BY HRH PRINCE ALBERT
IRONWORK: R. BROTHERHOOD, RAILWAY WORKS, CHIPPENHAM
ERECTION SUPERINTENDED BY DR. A. ROBERTSON,
BALMORAL ESTATES FACTOR

THIS PLAQUE WAS UNVEILED BY
HRH PRINCE PHILIP, DUKE OF EDINBURGH
ON 29TH MAY 2006
IN THE BICENTENARY YEAR OF BRUNEL'S BIRTH (1806)

PRESENTED
TO
Aberdeenshire
COUNCIL

PRESENTED
BY
ice

Albert, the Prince Consort - A Man of Science

Albert, Prince Consort
(Royal Collection Trust / © His Majesty King Charles III 2024)

Prince Albert was a man keen to observe the progress of science and industry and on his visit to Windsor in 1839 he had taken his first railway journey on 14 November, when on leaving Windsor, he had taken the train from Slough to Paddington. He was to take many rail journeys after that but like Victoria he was, on occasion, nervous of speed and conscious of the possibility of accidents in the early days of the railways, A newspaper of the time reported that in 1842 he said *not quite so fast next time, Mr Conductor, if you please.*

Prince Albert understood the importance of science and technology and in 1851 acted as Chairman of the Great Exhibition which *was a showcase for British technology, industry and art.* He attended the British Association for the Advancement of Science held in Ipswich in 1851 and in 1859 the Association invited him to be its President for the meeting to be held in Aberdeen in September. He was with the Queen at Balmoral and she wrote in her diary on 15 September: *I am very low spirited at my dearest Albert having to leave at one o' clock for Aberdeen to preside at the meeting of the British Association.*

The Prince travelled to Banchory by carriage and hence to Aberdeen by train to preside at the opening session of the twenty ninth meeting of the Association. It was held in the Music Hall, built especially for the event as a development of the existing Assembly Rooms. The week-long conference was so well attended that on the morning of the first day it had been necessary to stop the issue of associate tickets for the opening meeting that evening, despite the Music Hall having a capacity for two thousand seven hundred. The opening meeting had been arranged to start at 8.30 pm but every seat in the Music Hall had been taken shortly after the doors opened at 7 pm. The Prince spoke for about fifty minutes and his address was well received.

Aberdeen Music Hall – 1859 Meeting of the British Association

Alexander Thomson

He spent the night at Banchory House, Banchory-Devenick, as guest of Alexander Thomson, Convener of the County. He had inherited the property in 1806. In 1839 he had commissioned Aberdeen city architect John Smith, known as *Tudor Johnny*, to build the present house, possibly constructed on the foundations of a former residence dating from 1621. Within the grounds there is a monument to commemorate Prince Albert's visit to the house.

The following morning Prince Albert returned to the Music Hall and listened to presentations by some of the eminent scientists of the day attending the event - William Thomson, later Lord Kelvin; Sir William Rowan Hamilton, the mathematician; George Airy, the Astronomer Royal; Sir Charles Lyell, a champion of Charles Darwin's work on the theory of evolution; and the young Professor James Clerk Maxwell, Professor of Natural Philosophy at Aberdeen University. The Prince was also given a tour of Marischal College before leaving by train to return to Balmoral.

Monument on Tollohill
(Ewen Rennie)

Queen Victoria, once again, writes in her diary: *At ten minutes past seven arrived my beloved Albert. All had gone admirably; he had seen many learned people; all were delighted with his speech; the reception most gratifying. Banchory House (Mr Thomson's) where he lodged (four miles from Aberdeen) was, he said, very comfortable.*

The meeting concluded on Wednesday 21 September but on the following morning a party of almost two hundred members of the Association left Aberdeen at six o'clock for Balmoral Castle at the invitation of Her Majesty and the Prince Consort. They travelled by special train to Banchory and by carriage for the remainder of the journey. Meanwhile at Balmoral preparations were going ahead to prepare for their arrival.

The Queen records that *the morning dawned brightly. Suddenly a very high wind arose, which alarmed us, but yet it looked bright, and we hoped the wind would keep off the rain; but after breakfast, while watching he preparations, showers began, and from half past eleven a fearful down-pour, with that white curtain-like appearance which is so alarming; and this lasted till half past twelve. I was in despair; but at length it began to clear.*

The carriages carrying the members of the Association arrived at the castle shortly before two o'clock to the skirl of the pipes and a march past by some of the local families – the Farquharson men led by Colonel Farquharson, the Duffs by Lord Fife, and the Forbeses by Sir Charles Forbes of Newe. A Highland games was held including throwing the hammer, tossing the caber and putting the shot, watched by the Queen, Prince Albert, the Prince of Wales and other members of the royal family. This was followed by a *dejeuner served for members of the Association in the ballroom of the castle.* This was much needed by the visitors who had left Aberdeen early that morning without having taken breakfast. At six o'clock the party started on the homeward journey reaching, Aberdeen about one o'clock in the morning.

Queen Victoria records in her diary that *during the fete, we heard from Sir Roderick Murchison and others that news had been received this morning of the finding* (by Captain McClintock) *of poor Sir John Franklin's remains - or, rather, of the things belonging to him and his party.* Franklin's was a failed British voyage of Arctic exploration that departed England in 1845 aboard two ships and all trace had been lost, until then.
Sir Roderick Murchison, the eminent Scottish geologist, together with General Sabine, the retiring secretary of the Association,

Professor Phillips, the newly appointed secretary, and Mr Alexander Thomson of Banchory House were invited to stay that night at the castle and join the Queen and her other guests for dinner.

When the Queen journeyed north in 1860 she broke her journey at Edinburgh on 7 August to inspect over 21,000 Scottish volunteers who paraded in front of Arthur's Seat. These volunteers formed the forerunner of today's Territorial Army. She continued the following day to Balmoral and this was the first time she used the extension of the Deeside line to Aboyne, which had been opened in December 1859. The *Aberdeen Journal* reported that *the speed so far as Banchory was fast; but on coming to the new Deeside Extension line, upon which Her Majesty had not previously travelled, the rate of movement was slackened, and a series of views of scenery probably not equalled on any other railway were very satisfactorily obtained.* At Aboyne she was welcomed inside the station by the Second Company of Kincardineshire Volunteers and outside by a guard of honour provided by a company of the 93rd Highlanders. We are told that the noises of the engines of the royal train upset the horses of the awaiting royal carriage. They tried to bolt but all ended well and the carriage left with the Queen safely aboard on the last stage of the journey to Balmoral.

Prince Albert was only to enjoy two more summer holidays at Balmoral, the castle he had seen built and which he had so much enjoyed. He died of typhoid fever on 14 December 1861, aged 42, devastating Victoria so much that she entered into a deep state of mourning and wore black for the rest of her life.

The Unveiling of the Statue of Prince Albert in Aberdeen

One of Queen Victoria's first public engagements after the death of Prince Albert, was to unveil a statue of him in Aberdeen. On Thursday 14 October 1863 while the Queen and the family were at Balmoral, arrangements were made for her to travel to Aberdeen by train. She was extremely nervous and wrote in her diary: *longed not to have to go through this fearful ordeal.* Victoria and Albert had nine of a family - Victoria (known as Vicky), Albert, Alice, Alfred, Helena (known as Lenchen), Louise, Arthur, Leopold and Beatrice and several of them accompanied her. She wrote: *I started sad and lonely, and so strange without my darling, with dear Alice, Lenchen and Louise.* At Aboyne she met up with Vicky and her husband Fritz of Prussia, Alice's husband Louis of Hesse and three of her sons, Arthur and Leopold, who had gone on ahead. Alfred met them at Aberdeen having come that morning by train from Edinburgh. Beatrice was left at home - she was only six. The Queen's eldest son Albert, later to be King Edward VII, was not at Balmoral at the time.

The preparations for her arrival at Aberdeen were simple and respectful of the occasion. *Two huge flags were suspended across the inside entrance and the floor of the passage leading into the portico was laid with crimson cloth.* There to meet the Queen and her family was the Duke of Richmond, Alexander Anderson, Provost of Aberdeen, and various other local dignitaries, The weather was far from pleasant for the drive from the station to the site for the new statue. The procession went by way of Guild Street, Regent Quay, Marischal Street, Castle Street and Union Street to the corner of Union Terrace. The weather was far from pleasant but that did not deter large crowds lining the route but remaining silent and respectful.

Regarding the spot where the statue was placed, the Queen said that it was *rather small, and on one side close to the bridge but that the sculptor Baron Carlo Marochetti had chosen it himself.* She was not impressed when she alighted from her carriage that *no one was there to direct me and to say, as formerly, what was to be done. Oh! it was and is too painful, too dreadful!*

Unveiling of Prince Albert's statue in Aberdeen

Before the unveiling the royal party, perhaps because of the inclement weather, gathered in the Northern Assurance building on the corner of Union Terrace. The choice of venue was no doubt the work of the Provost, Alexander Anderson, a prominent advocate in the city. Among his non-legal activities, he had set up the Aberdeen Fire and Life Assurance company in 1836, renamed the Northern Assurance Company in 1848. The provost handed her his address in which he paid tribute to the Prince Consort's *brightest display of intellectual and moral greatness* and in turn the Queen handed over her reply. In it she wrote *it was with feelings which I fail in seeking words to express that I determined to attend here today to witness the inauguration of the statue which will record to future times the love and respect of the people of this county and city for my great and beloved husband.* Sir George Grey, the Queen's private secretary, then commanded the provost to kneel and taking the sword from Sir George, the Queen touched the provost on each shoulder and said *Arise Sir Alexander Anderson.*

With that part of the ceremony completed, the royal party left the building and proceeded, in the pouring rain, to the platform for the unveiling. First there was a prayer by Principal Campbell who, we are told, spoke for ten minutes. Her Majesty more than once betrayed signs of impatience but did record in her diary that night that, although *Principal Campbell's prayer was very long - which was trying in the rain - part of it (since I have read it) is really very good.* The statue was then unveiled and after a brief viewing the Queen and the royal party retired to the Northern Assurance building where lunch was served. Just before three o'clock the procession made its way back to the station for the return journey to Aboyne and on by carriage to Balmoral.

Prince Albert statue in Aberdeen
(Royal Collection Trust / © His Majesty King Charles III 2024)

The statue shows the Prince seated in the uniform of a Field Marshal and wearing the insignia of the Order of the Thistle, the highest honour of Scotland. It remained at the corner of Union Terrace until 1914 when it was decided that it be moved to allow a new statue of

King Edward VII, who had died in 1910, to be erected on the spot. There was much discussion on a suitable place for the statue of Prince Albert but it was finally agreed that it be placed in the garden area on Rosemount Viaduct, opposite His Majesty's Theatre.

On 20 March 2014 the *Aberdeen Journal* carried a letter from a correspondent that on the first Sunday after the statue had been relocated to its new position, he had noted that those attending the services in the city church of St Nicholas saw, to their astonishment, that someone had stuck an old battered silk hat on Prince Albert's s bare head to protect it from the rain - much to the amusement of the passersby.

Mention of the Northern Assurance building reminds us that generations of Aberdonians would say *meet you at the Monkey House* the name given to this building. It is believed it earned its name from the pillars in the portico, people believing it looked like the bars in a zoo with the monkeys standing in behind waiting to meet their loved ones at this prominent location.

Statue of Queen Victoria in Aberdeen

Soon after the unveiling in 1863 of Prince Albert's statue at a meeting of the royal tradesmen of Aberdeen, one of its members, Alexander Donald, made the proposal that a statue in marble of Her Majesty Queen Victoria be erected and made the suggestion that the corner of St Nicholas Street would be a perfect setting. In May of that year the fine Italian renaissance style building, originally constructed for the Town and County Bank, opened for business and made an excellent background for the statue. A fundraising committee of prominent citizens took up the challenge and appointed a local man, Alexander Brodie, as sculptor. He submitted a photograph of his proposal, showing the Queen full length in court robe. The Queen, however, considered the statue should show her as a Scottish Queen and show her in Scottish regal attire fastened by a thistle brooch. Her detailed instructions even indicated the dispersal of the drapery on the back of the figure. The statue stands on a substantial plinth of pink Peterhead granite with the inscription:

Victoria, D.G. Britanniarum Regina 1866. As originally suggested, the statue was placed in the angle at the junction of St Nicholas Street and Union Street. The space had had to be bridged over the roadway 6 metres below and a pier built to support the statue and plinth.

On 20 September 1866 Albert Edward, Prince of Wales, travelled from Abergeldie Castle where he was in residence with his wife Alexandra and family. He travelled by carriage to Ballater and then by special train to Guild Street station. This was the first time Ballater station had been used - the official opening was not until a month later. He was accompanied by General William Knollys, Treasurer and Comptroller to the Household, Col William Keppel, his Equerry and Dr Andrew Robertson, Royal Commissioner at Balmoral. The Prince was welcomed by the Lord Provost, Sir Alexander Anderson, who conferred on him the freedom of the city, attaching the scroll to the Prince's Glengarry cap. Also present were Lord Derby, the Prime Minister, who had arrived earlier by the mail train; Principal Campbell and members of the Senatus of the University; Lord Kintore, Lord Lieutenant of the County of Aberdeen; and Sir James Horn Burnett of Leys, Lord Lieutenant of Kincardineshire. With the welcome completed, the procession made its way to the site of the statue through crowd-lined streets bedecked in flags and bunting. His Royal Highness the Prince took his place on a platform with William Leslie, chairman of subscribers - who read his address and invited the Prince to unveil the statue covered in the Royal standard.

In his reply the Prince said, *Gentlemen, it has afforded me the greatest satisfaction to attend here today, by the wish of Her Majesty, and at your invitation, for the purpose of inaugurating a statue of the Queen, my dear mother. Her Majesty has desired me to express to you how much she appreciates the motives which have led the people of Aberdeenshire to give this lasting evidence of their attachment and loyalty to her person, of which she has so many proofs, and whose sympathy in her great sorrow has touched her so deeply. Her Majesty's satisfaction is much enhanced by the cordial unanimity which has combined all classes of your city and county in the erection of a work so grateful to her Majesty's feelings and one so satisfactory as a work of art. On my own part I have to thank you Gentlemen for your expressions of attachment you have been good enough to make use of towards myself and the Princess of Wales and the other members of the royal family and I heartily desire to join in your prayer that Her Majesty may long be spared to reign over a happy, loyal and devoted people.*

Alexander Brodie, the sculptor, was introduced to the Prince who commended him on his work which he considered a very good likeness. The Prince then went with the Lord Provost Sir Alexander Anderson to his house for lunch, but before leaving by train for Ballater and thence Abergeldie at 4 pm, the Prince paid a visit to the Autumn Show of the Royal Horticultural Society in the Music Hall.

Unveiling Queen Victoria's statue in Aberdeen.

The following Monday the Prince, this time accompanied by his wife and two sons, travelled from Ballater to the station at Guild Street in Aberdeen, where they transferred to Waterloo Station in

London, then a station of the Great North of Scotland Railway. There they joined a train taking them to Dunrobin Castle where they were guests of the Duke of Sutherland.

The Aberdeen Town and County Bank.
G. W. Wilson   Aberdeen

The Queen's Statue, Aberdeen.
G. W. Wilson   Aberdeen

After a few years, Queen Victoria's marble statue began to show weathering due to the frost and so it was moved to the vestibule of the Town House in 1888, where it remains to this day. It stands at the foot of the splendid main stairway. A plaster model of Brodie's statue has also been on display in the Music Hall for many years. A new bronze statue of an older Victoria was commissioned by the royal tradesmen of the city to commemorate Her Majesty's Golden Jubilee in 1887. The sculptor was Charles Bell Birch. It was erected at the St Nicholas Street location on 9 November 1893. Known as *The Queen* it became a regular meeting place for generations of Aberdonians.

To make way for the extension of Marks & Spencer, the 1893 statue moved to its current site at Queen's Cross on 22 January 1964. Victoria now stands looking west towards Balmoral.

Opening of the Waterworks at Invercannie

On 16 October 1866 Queen Victoria opened the new waterworks at Invercannie. The supply of water was formerly taken from the river Dee at the old Bridge of Dee about two miles from the town; but the need for a better supply than that afforded by the Bridge of Dee works had long been a matter of concern. *The London Illustrated News* reported that the town had extended largely to the westward on ground ly*ing higher than the pumping could supply and the greatest scarcity has often prevailed during the day causing housewives having to lay in a supply during the night for service during the day.* In 1861 Alexander Anderson, Provost of Aberdeen, called a meeting of the citizens to decide whether a supply of water should be brought to the town from Cairnton. It was approved by a large majority and work started in 1864. Queen Victoria had been well briefed on the extent of the scheme and wrote in her diary: *These waterworks are on a most extensive scale and are estimated to convey to the city 6,000,000 gallons of water daily: The water is from the River Dee, from which it is diverted at Cairnton, about four miles above Banchory. The principal features of the works are a tunnel 760 yards in length, which is cut through the hill of Cairnton, composed of solid rock of a very hard nature. At the end of the tunnel is the Invercannie Reservoir where the ceremony took place. This reservoir is estimated to contain 15,000,000 gallons of water. It is just two years and a half since the first turf of this undertaking was cut, and the cost of the works is £130,000.* From Invercannie the water was to be taken by way of an aqueduct, constructed of brick, about 31 km in length, to a reservoir at Mannofield in Aberdeen.

On the day of the opening, Tuesday 16 October 1866, the Queen left Balmoral by carriage, just before ten o'clock, accompanied by her daughters Helena and Louise, followed in a second carriage by Christian, Helena's husband Arthur, the Duchess of Roxburgh - who the Queen described as a *dear and valued friend* - and Lady Emily Cathcart, her lady-in-waiting. There to meet the royal party were Colonel Farquharson, Chairman of the Aboyne and Braemar Railway Company, and John Duncan, Chairman of the Deeside Railway Company.

The Queen was invited to board the special train which left Ballater just after 11 am. This was the first time the station had been used by the Queen - the official opening was the following day. Captain Tyler of the Board of Trade was not satisfied with the state of two bridges on the route and as a temporary measure had propped up the girders. He then wrote to Sir Stafford Northcote, the President of the Board of Trade, informing him of his actions: *I think it is right to tell you of this. If you should hear of a bridge being propped up you will know the reason. But you need not be under any apprehension as regards the Queen going over the line on Tuesday, and it may still be opened as proposed for public traffic on Wednesday.*

After a pleasant run Inchmarlo was reached at 11.58 am. Here a temporary platform had been erected and on alighting from the train, Her Majesty was received by Sir James Burnett, Lord Lieutenant of Kincardineshire and Mr Patrick Davidson of Inchmarlo. Inchmarlo had become known to the Queen on her first visit to Deeside in 1848 when along with Prince Albert and her family she had journeyed up the valley to Balmoral. After the opening of the railway to Banchory in 1853 and until the railway was extended to Aboyne in 1859, the Queen, we are told, ordered her coachman to drive through the Inchmarlo estate because she so loved the gardens. The Queen, in an open carriage drawn by four greys, was taken by the west gate of the policies of Inchmarlo and then via the Cairnton road entering Invercannie from the west.

Inchmarlo House, Banchory

West Gate at Inchmarlo

The ceremony had been arranged for 4 pm but it was reported that *three days before, her Majesty thoughtfully sent word to the Lord Provost that as this hour would probably be rather late, the time might be changed to twelve noon - an alteration which gave general satisfaction.*

Lord Provost Sir Alexander Anderson accompanied by Lady Anderson, had come by carriage from Aberdeen and were joined by the Police Commissioners and a large number of Aberdeen citizens who had left Aberdeen by a first regular train of the Deeside Railway, arriving at Banchory about nine in the morning. Having reached Banchory, transport to Invercannie had been arranged. They were joined by local people until over a thousand awaited the arrival of their Queen who was to be welcomed by the Lord Provost. From there transport to Invercannie had been arranged.

The ceremony lasted about fifteen minutes - the Lord Provost read his address and the Queen responded: *I thank you for your dutiful address and am very sensible of this fresh mark of the loyal attachment of my neighbours, the people of Aberdeen. I have felt that, at a time when the attention of the country has been so seriously directed to the state of the public health, it was right that I should make the exertion to testify my sense of the importance of a work so well calculated as this to promote the health and comfort of your ancient city.*

She then turned the stopcock which saw the water rushing up. The royal party left by the same route, stopping briefly at Patrick Davidson's house to be presented with flowers by his daughter. The Queen records that she was back at Balmoral by twenty minutes past two. She wrote in her diary that it *made me feel very nervous; but I got through it well, though it was the first time I had read anything since my darling Husband was taken from me.*

In the Queen's speech she refers to *My Neighbours the people of Aberdeen* which prompted William Carnie to write a poem recalling the day:

'Twas a merry morn at Cairnton, a festive day, I trow
When there our Queen, in graceful speech, bade Dee's bright water flow;
The cheers rang through the woods around, as 'mid the autumn scene
Sir Alexander bowed his best for -
My Neighbours of Aberdeen

To this day Aberdeen's water supply still comes from Invercannie although it is now supplemented by a second cast-iron pipeline. Work on this started in 1920 and was completed in 1926 and inaugurated on 30 September that year, by Princess Arthur of Connaught, Duchess of Fife, granddaughter of King Edward VII.

Note:

The title Lord Provost of Aberdeen was formally established in 1863 when Queen Victoria knighted Sir Alexander Anderson designing him *Lord Provost of Aberdeen*. In 2022, a successor in office, Lord Provost James (Barney) Crockett said of him: *Alexander Anderson shaped our city in some of the most obvious ways; what we see at the harbour now, the water supply and the health improvements which helped the population grow, installing Aberdeen's great history in caring for women. Not forgetting Anderson Drive, that has his name, pushing out the city. It's all part of his legacy.*

In August 1899 saw the constitution of the city of Aberdeen *as a county of a city* by Queen Victoria. Following this, the office of Lord Lieutenant was established in Aberdeen and linked to the office of Lord Provost. The Lord Lieutenant is the monarch's first representative within the city boundary with a principal duty to represent the Crown within the Lieutenancy area and to uphold its dignity. In practical terms this means facilitating royal visits, promoting the honours system and liaising with the armed forces.

The Queen at Balmoral after the Death of Prince Albert

After the death of Prince Albert in December 1861 Queen Victoria started to visit her Highland home twice a year, first in the spring and then for an extended period in the autumn. The east coast route had been used previously by Queen Victoria but she now started using the west coast route still using Ferryhill as the terminus where the engine was reversed to take the train initially to Aboyne, which had opened in 1859, and from 1867 to Ballater. For this part of the journey the sending of a pilot engine ahead of the royal train was dispensed with but other precautions were observed: level crossing gates were closed fifteen minutes ahead of the time the train was due and station platforms were closed to the public. The Queen had a dislike for high speed and no attempt was ever made to reduce the journey time from Ferryhill to Ballater which took 75 minutes at speeds never exceeding 64 km/h (40 miles per hour). When travelling at night, which was the usual practice on her journeys to and from London, the Queen preferred the train not to exceed 48 km/h (30 miles per hour). On one occasion the Queen sent John Brown down the platform when the royal train had stopped with a message to the driver to slow down. Brown added in his strong local accent: *Her Maa-dj-esty says the carriage is shakin' like the Deil.*

The royal train had been made up of a number of saloon cars and luggage cars provided by the London and North Western Railway company but in 1869 she commissioned that company to build two coaches for her exclusive use. The cost of £700 was paid personally by the Queen and the coaches were painted using 23-carat gold paint with various royal coats of arms on the lower panels and the interiors lined in silk and satins. Queen Victoria was extremely proud of her accommodation and the two coaches were the first to be fitted with a flexible gangway linking the two. It provided the Queen with her day and night accommodation and the second bed in the Queen's sleeping apartment was often used by one of the royal princesses. The Queen disliked having a meal on a moving train and insisted that refreshments be served at a convenient point on the route. Her carriages had no connection to the rest of the train which meant that if the Queen required the services of her staff they had to climb down from their carriage when there was no platform using the footboards - not ideal on a dark night or at some remote spot. Initially there was no electric light, the Queen preferring oil lamps and even when electric was introduced, she insisted that the old fittings should remain. Another upgrade was the installation of an onboard toilet which the Queen was reluctant to use, preferring the train to stop for toilet breaks. In 1897 the two carriages were rebuilt united on one frame, dispensing with the flexible gangway which better suited the Queen, as it made it much easier for her to move between her day and night accommodation.

Royal carriage after 1897 upgrade.

While at Balmoral, the Queen used the train for royal engagements - in 1863 to unveil the statue of Prince Albert in Aberdeen and in 1866 to open Aberdeen's waterworks at Invercannie. She also used the train for private visits which took her to see the beauties of the countryside of Scotland. Often it gave the Queen the opportunity of revisiting parts of her kingdom that she had visited with Prince Albert when they enjoyed many expeditions on horseback. Her visits by train were to become a regular part of her autumn holiday at Balmoral.

The Queen was always accompanied by family members, her doctor, private secretary, ladies in waiting and usually John Brown her *faithful servant.* He was born at Crathienaird, near Balmoral, on 2 December 1827. Brown was the son of a farmer who had also been a schoolteacher and when John was five the family moved to Bush. John, the second son, began work at the age of thirteen as an outdoor servant at Balmoral, which Queen Victoria and Prince Albert leased in

John Brown

February 1848, and purchased outright in November 1851. He then permanently entered the royal service and by good conduct and intelligence, he gradually rose, and was appointed, in 1858, the Queen's personal servant in Scotland; this appointment was, in February 1865, extended to wherever Her Majesty might be.

On 15 September 1863 accompanied by Princess Helena, Victoria travelled from Aboyne to Perth where she stopped for breakfast. She left the train at the small station of Blair Atholl and made her way to Blair Castle, the home of the Duke of Atholl, who was terminally ill. Six years later on 1 September1869, along with Princesses Louise and Beatrice, she went by carriage to Ballater and joined the train which took her to Callander to spend ten days exploring the Trossachs.

In October 1870 the Marquis of Lorne, while out walking at Glassalt Shiel, the Queen's favourite retreat after the death of Prince Albert, proposed to Princess Louise. On returning later to Balmoral she surprised her mother by announcing her engagement. The Queen recorded: *Though I was not unprepared for this result, I felt painfully the thought of losing her.*

On 6 September 1872 the Queen was able to use her new, specially commissioned railway carriage to visit the Duke of Sutherland. With Prince Leopold and Princess Beatrice, she left Ballater on 6 September 1872 on her way first to Aberdeen and then north, finally reaching Golspie. She was the guest of the Duke at Dunrobin Castle and returned to Balmoral overnight on 11 September. The following year, along with Princess Beatrice she left Ballater on 9 September for Aberdeen and then south to Stanley Junction (just north of Perth) where her train joined the Highland Railway to Kingussie. She was to spend the next seven days exploring Inverlochy, returning from Inverness on the 16 September. Two years later on 21 September 1875 and once again with Princess Beatrice, she set off on another journey. Her train took her from Ballater to Tyndrum where she went by carriage to Inveraray Castle to be the guest of the Duke and Duchess of Argyll. Their son, the Marquis of Lorne, had married Princess Louise in 1871 and they were there to greet the Queen. She was to spend time exploring the area and returned to Balmoral on 29 September. From the 12-18 September 1877 the Queen, with Princess Beatrice, had an expedition to Loch Maree. They travelled by train from Ballater, passing through Aberdeen and on to Inverness, where they left the train at the small station at Achnasheen and then travelled by carriage to Gairloch which was the base for her visit to this part of Scotland.

Her large family were regular visitors to Balmoral and it was the place where royal marriages were arranged. In 1855 Prince Frederick Wilhelm of Prussia came to ask the Queen and Prince Albert for the hand in marriage of Victoria, the Princess Royal. They married two years later and in October 1863 they returned with their son Prince Wilhelm to visit the Queen at Balmoral.

The Crown Prince of Prussia (1831-88), later Frederick III,
Emperor of Germany and his son, Prince William (1859-1941),
later Kaiser Wilhelm II at Balmoral.

The journeys to and from Scotland were almost invariably overnight. In June 1873 on her way south, the Queen said she wanted to read in bed before going to sleep. It was discovered that the oil lamps were dry and her servant John Brown reported the deficiency in forthright terms to the superintendent of LNWR, who was travelling on the train: *The Queen says the train shanna stir a fut till the lamps are put in.* A special stop had to be made to remedy the situation!

On 29 August 1874 the Queen went by carriage to the station at Ballater to greet her son Prince Alfred, Duke of Edinburgh, and his bride Princess Marie, Grand Duchess of Russia. The marriage was at the Winter Palace in St Petersburg on 23 January 1874, and directly united the British and Russian royal families for the first time. Queen Victoria was unable to attend the celebrations, and remained at Osborne house, but clearly felt the day was important. She therefore was particularly pleased to welcome them to Balmoral and to be joined for the occasion by other members of the family - Princess Helena, Prince Leopold and Princess Beatrice.

On 17 September 1875 the Queen, Prince Albert the Prince of Wales and his wife Princess Alexandra, then staying at Abergeldie Castle, were at dinner that night with the Queen at Balmoral on the eve of their departure for India. The Queen was anxious the visit should be a success and talked with them over various details of the journey. In her diary she wrote *It was very sad to see him drive off with Alix and the boys (the little girls followed in another carriage), not knowing what might happen, or if he would ever return. May God bless him!*

The Prince carried out an extensive tour of India before returning home in May 1876. With the passing of the Royal Titles Act of 1876, Queen Victoria took the title Empress of India from 1 May 1876.

Prince Arthur, Duke of Connaught, had married Princess Louise Margaret of Prussia in March 1879 and they came to visit the Queen on 5 September that year. The Queen and Princess Beatrice went to Ballater station for their homecoming and accompanied them by carriage to Balmoral. In her diary Queen Victoria wrote: *When we reached the Balmoral bridge, we went at a slow pace passing under the arch composed of moss and heather, on which was wrought, in flowers, 'Welcome to Balmoral' on one side and 'Ceud mille Failte' on the other.*

The following day the Duke of Connaught's cairn was unveiled on a nearby hill overlooking the castle and on a stone was inscribed -

ARTHUR, DUKE OF CONNAUGHT AND STRATHEARN,
Married to Princess Louise Margaret of Prussia,
March 13, 1879

Prince Leopold, Duke of Albany, and his wife Princess Helena of Waldeck-Pyrmont
(Royal Collection Trust
© His Majesty King Charles III 2024)

On 13 September 1882 the Queen, accompanied by her daughter Princess Beatrice, were once again at Ballater station to greet her son Prince Leopold, Duke of Albany, and his wife Princess Helena of Waldeck-Pyrmont. The marriage was at Windsor earlier in that year but sadly it was not to last long; Prince Leopold, who was haemophilic, died in 1884. Also, at Balmoral to greet Leopold, was his sister-in-law, Princess Louise, wife of his brother Arthur. That day, news had been received of the decisive victory at Tel-el-Kebir in the Anglo-Egyptian conflict and the part played in the battle by Prince Arthur.

The only member of the Queen's family still unmarried was her youngest daughter, Princess Beatrice. The Queen was so set against her youngest daughter marrying that she refused to discuss the possibility. Nevertheless, many suitors were suggested, including Louis Napoleon, Prince Imperial, the son of the exiled Emperor Napoleon III of France. Beatrice was attracted to him but it all came to an extremely sad end when he was killed in the Anglo-Zulu War in 1879. Beatrice was at Balmoral with the Queen on 19 June when news was received of his death. The Queen was finishing her holiday the following day and along with Beatrice they left from Ballater the following afternoon. On this occasion the Queen took the east coast route south in order see the ill-fated Tay bridge which had opened on 1 June 1878. The royal train stopped at Tay Bridge Station and Thomas Bouch, the designer of the bridge, was invited to board the train to meet the Queen.

The Queen and Princess
Beatrice 1878
(Royal Collection Trust
© His Majesty
King Charles III 2024)

The train then crossed the bridge at a reduced speed *of 15 mph to allow the royal visitors to enjoy the magnificent view.* A month later the Queen conferred a knighthood on Thomas Bouch. It was not to prove his finest moment as on 29 December 1879, a very stormy night, the bridge was destroyed. A train which was on the bridge plunged into the Tay with a loss of eighty passengers.

When the Queen returned to Balmoral in the autumn of 1879, she invited the grieving Eugenie, Louis Napoleon's mother, to come north and stay at Abergeldie *for a little quiet and change of air after the terrible loss of your son.* In 1870, her husband Napoleon III had capitulated to the Prussians marking the end of the Franco-Prussian war. He died in 1873 and Eugénie and her son were forced to flee France and live in exile in Britain.

Beatrice fell in love with Prince Henry of Battenberg. Finally, the Queen agreed and they married in 1885 on condition that Beatrice and Henry make their home with her and that Beatrice continue her duties as the Queen's unofficial secretary. Duthie Park in Aberdeen was gifted to the city by Miss Elizabeth Crombie Duthie of Ruthrieston. It had been hoped that the Queen would open the park but she was recovering from an accident. Instead, it was left to Princess Beatrice to attend the ceremony. She left from Ballater on the Royal train on 27 September 1883 and went first to the Aberdeen Joint Station. From there she travelled by carriage to open a bazaar in aid of the Sick Children's Hospital and thence to formally open the Duthie Park. Despite the wet and windy day, she toured the park before returning to Balmoral from a specially constructed platform near the mound.

Princess Beatrice opening Duthie Park on a very rainy day.

Group photograph at Balmoral of Queen Victoria (1819-1901) with
Prince Albert Victor of Wales (1864-1892); Princess Beatrice (1857-1944);
Princess Victoria of Wales (1868-1935); The Duchess of Edinburgh;
the Crown Princess of Prussia; Princess Louise of Wales; Princess Victoria of
Prussia; Princess Alexandra of Edinburgh; Princess Maud of Wales;
Princess Victoria Melita of Edinburgh and Princess Marie of Edinburgh
(Royal Collection Trust / © His Majesty King Charles III 2024)

Messenger Trains

Until 1864, whenever the Queen was at Balmoral, her private mail and the red government Despatch Boxes, guarded by a courier, came by train to Perth and then by pony and trap across the hills and the Devil's Elbow to the castle - a most hazardous journey in those days. Barrow Hepburn & Gale, the makers of these boxes today, suggest two reasons for the use of red as the predominant colour of the boxes. One is that Prince Albert preferred the colour because it was the predominant one on the arms of the House of Saxe-Coburg-Gotha. A more colourful explanation is that the practice dates from the late sixteenth century, when Queen Elizabeth I's representative, Francis Throckmorton, presented the Spanish ambassador, Bernardino de Mendoza, with a specially-constructed red briefcase filled with black puddings! It was seen as the official communication from the Queen and so the colour red became the official colour of the state.

In the summer of 1864, it occurred to the Deeside Railway Company that as the Queen was using the company, it could offer a service for her mail. The secretary of the company, William B Ferguson, wrote to General Charles Grey, the Queen's Private Secretary, with the proposal. It was agreed and the service started on 8 October 1865. The only stops were at Banchory and Aboyne so that it could collect the Queen's mail and despatch boxes from the overnight train from London to Aberdeen and initially take them by train to Aboyne and later, when the line was extended, to Ballater. We are told that this meant that any note from her Prime Minister would be with her the following morning - quite an achievement for transport at that time. The company's charge was set at £9 2s 0d per day for the return journey and that included the courier's breakfast and the cost of the carriage from terminus to the castle. After delivering the mail and despatch boxes the train returned to Aberdeen in the afternoon in time to connect with the night train.

The coach of the train for the courier was painted gold and purple with the royal cypher. It has also been claimed that the engine was unique, painted all over with the reds, blues and whites of the Royal Stewart dress pattern. It must have been quite a sight as it made its way along the track. After a short time the engine was repainted, still in tartan, but in the quieter hues of the Duff plaid. The tartan engine was taken off the route during World War I and repainted in dull colours and demoted to a branch line and renamed *Meldrum Meg*. Mr W A Mitchell writing in *Deeside Field* in 1966 claims that it was last seen standing idle in a railway yard at Inverurie.

Later a second coach was added to accommodate VIPs, often including one of the Queen's ministers. Early on, what became Messenger Trains ran only on weekdays except Mondays. When, in 1870 a Sunday service was added, this did not meet with the approval of those who considered trains should not run on the Lord's Day. Messengers only ran when the Queen was in residence, but the timetables were shown for many years in Bradshaw and the train was available to first-class passengers and their servants paying third-class fares.

In 1873 the Queen wrote to her Prime Minister, William Gladstone, complaining that the messenger train was repeatedly running late - *the post never comes in two days running at the same time. In short it has come to pass that the Government must consider what penalties should be imposed.*

Prime Ministers William Gladstone and Benjamin Disraeli
(Royal Collection Trust / © His Majesty King Charles III 2024)

The years between 1867 and 1885 are mostly known for two great, and contending, prime ministers - the Conservative Benjamin Disraeli, and the Liberal William Gladstone. Victoria's relationship with the former was very good; the latter she disliked immensely.

Both, at various times, had to make the journey north to Aberdeen on the night train and then by the Messenger to Ballater.

Benjamin Disraeli became Prime Minister for the second time in 1874 but was clearly exasperated and complained that *carrying on the government of the country 600 miles from the metropolis doubles the labour.* That year he had turned ill when on a visit to Balmoral; the Queen offered him a peerage, but he was reluctant to leave the House of Commons for the Lords.

On Monday 15 September 1884 William Gladstone left Balmoral, where he had been with the Queen, and joined the Messenger train for Aberdeen. When the train reached Banchory there was another in the station in which the Prince of Wales was travelling. The crowd that had gathered recognised the Prince, and gave the usual loyal cheers but Gladstone received a tremendous ovation. He had been touring Scotland to gain support for a bill, the Representation of the People Act, which had been rejected by the House of Lords. He used the opportunity to speak to the people. Gladstone resigned as Prime Minister in June 1885 when he failed to gain a majority in the General Election

Lord Salisbury possibly travelled on the Messenger train to Ballater to have an audience with the Queen on Saturday 13 June when she invited him to form a government. Lord Salisbury referred to the visit as being sent for with a vengeance, loathing the journey to a place he always called Siberia!

The only other occasion a change of Prime Minister has taken place at Balmoral was two days before the death of Queen Elizabeth II when on 6 October 2022, Liz Truss was invited to form a government. She announced her intention to resign after only forty-four days.

The Messengers continued running, except during the years of World War I when the King did not come to Balmoral, until 1937, when it was considered that a special train service was unnecessary. The courier once again made the journey by road between Perth and Balmoral.

The original station of 1853 at Crathes had been a private halt for Sir Robert Burnett of Leys and was situated close to the gate leading to the castle. Ten years later the laird gave land for the building of a new station on the understanding that all trains would stop at Crathes. Clearly this was not happening and after much correspondence the messenger trains started calling at Crathes. In 1882, however, the Great North of Scotland Railway, which had taken over the Deeside Railway, introduced a Saturday half-day excursion to Ballater stopping only at Banchory and Aboyne.

ON SATURDAY AFTERNOONS,

UNTIL FURTHER NOTICE,

A FAST EXCURSION TRAIN

WILL BE RUN FROM ABERDEEN TO

BANCHORY, ABOYNE, & BALLATER.

FARES—THERE AND BACK.

BANCHORY, First Class, 2s. 0d.; Third Class, 1s. 3d.
ABOYNE, } Do. 4s. 0d. Do. 2s. 0d.
BALLATER, }

The Train will leave ABERDEEN at 1 o'clock, P.M., and return from BALLATER at 8 o'clock, P.M., ABOYNE at 8·20 P.M., and BANCHORY at 8·50 P.M., arriving in ABERDEEN about 9·30 P.M.

COACH ARRANGEMENTS.

In connection with the Excursion Train, Mr. MACGREGOR, Invercauld Arms, Ballater, will run an Open Coach from Ballater Station, up the north side of the River Dee by the Bridge of Gairn and Coil-a-Creich to Crathie; returning via Balmoral and the south side of the Dee, affording Passengers a fine view of Abergeldie Castle and the Deer Forest of Birkhall, and arriving at Ballater at 7 p.m.

Fare for the Coach Journey of nearly Twenty Miles, 2/6.

As the number of Coach Passengers will be limited, early application should be made for Tickets, which are obtainable in Aberdeen only.

TICKET ARRANGEMENTS.

Tickets for these Excursions, and for the Coach in connection, may be had, on and after Wednesday of each week, at MURRAY'S TICKET OFFICES, Union Street, Aberdeen, and at the COMPANY'S BOOKING OFFICE, Joint Station.

The Special Excursion Tickets are only available by the Trains named. No Luggage allowed.

Sir Robert was not pleased. The company claimed that the excursion trains had appeared by mistake in the timetable and were not available for ordinary fare-paying passengers. In 1883 Sir Robert took his case to the Court of Session in Edinburgh for a ruling - which he lost but won the judgement on appeal to the House of Lords two years later. Lord Bramwell ruled that whereas excursion trains would not have to stop at Crathes the messengers and other timetabled trains would require to make a stop. Under the terms of the feu charter this was followed until 1914 when Sir Thomas Burnett of Leys agreed to waive his rights resulting in some fast regular trains no longer having to make a stop at Crathes.

The Queen's neighbours at Mar Lodge

The Mar Lodge estate was part of the Earldom of Mar. John Erskine, 6th Earl of Mar, known as *Bobbing John* because of his tendency to move from one cause to another, forfeited the estate in 1716 because of his support for the Jacobite uprising. Ownership of the land passed to the Earls of Fife and in the years that followed, the large estates of Invercauld and Mar bought up all the smaller lairdships until they were the only two estates in Braemar. In the nineteenth century they were mainly used for shooting and fishing and attracted the wealthy to come to enjoy the sport. The first hunting lodge was damaged by the *Muckle Spate* of 1829 but was repaired and by 1849 was described as *a commodious hunting-seat of the Earl of Fife's and that it was being rented, with the adjoining deer forests, by the Duke of Leeds*.

The original Mar Lodge

Francis Osborne, Marquess of Carmarthen, had taken a lease of Mar forest and had become a great supporter of the Braemar Gathering, becoming an honorary member of the Society. One of his subsidiary titles was Viscount Dunblane and so enthusiastic was he that he provided his retainers with full Dunblane tartan. In 1836 he presided at the Gathering when both the Earl of Fife and Mr Farquharson were out of the county. He became 7th Duke of Leeds two years later.

The popularity of the Braemar Gathering was becoming the event of the summer season and in 1843 it was noted that it was attended by *most of the nobility and gentry wearing full highland dress.* That year it had a royal visitor when Prince Alexander of the Netherlands attended as guest of the Duke of Leeds and the following year he had as a guest His Serene Highness Prince Edward of Saxe-Weimar. The Duke died in 1859.

James Duff, the 4th Earl of Fife, used Corriemulzie Cottage on the south side of the Dee, west of the Falls of Corriemulzie as a summer residence. It had been built about 1825 by the Earl's brother, General Sir Alexander Duff. Originally of modest scale, as one writer said, with *no pretension to being more than a highland shooting box,* it was developed and enlarged into what became known as New Mar Lodge.

In September 1852 Queen Victoria and Prince Albert attended a ball at Corriemulzie given by James Duff and his wife Agnes. James became 5th Earl of Fife in 1857 on the death of his uncle. In her diary the Queen wrote: *We dined at a quarter past six o'clock and at seven started for Corriemulzie for a torchlight ball in the open air. We arrived there at half past eight, by which time, of course, it was dark. Mr and Lady Agnes Duff received us at the door, and then took us at once through the house to the open space where the ball was, which was hid from our view till the curtains were drawn asunder. It was really a beautiful and most unusual sight. All the company were assembled there. A space about one hundred feet in length and sixty feet in width, was boarded, and entirely surrounded by Highlanders bearing torches, which were placed in sockets, and constantly replenished. I must not omit to mention a reel danced by eight Highlanders holding torches in their hands.*

CORRIEMULZIE COTTAGE.

The Queen and Prince left Corriemulzie at half past nine and were back at the old Balmoral castle by just after eleven.

Alexander Duff inherited the title of the 6th Earl of Fife on the death of his father in 1879 and ten years later he was created 1st Duke of Fife on his marriage to Princess Louise, eldest daughter of the future King Edward VII. Their home, New Mar Lodge, was lost in a fire in 1895.

Later that year, on 15 October, Queen Victoria laid the foundation stone of their new home close to the site of the earlier Mar Lodge on the north side of the Dee. The building was completed in 1898.

Rebuilt Mar Lodge, September 1898
(Royal Collection Trust / © His Majesty King Charles III 2024)

Queen Victoria died in 1901 but Mar Lodge and the part played over the years by the Deeside Railway lived on.

The Braemar Gathering drew large crowds. The largest ever attendance during her reign was in 1898, when it was held at Balmoral. According to the *Aberdeen Journal* the crowd numbered 14,000 - 15,000 *larger and more fashionable than ever before.* People had travelled, not only from the surrounding area, but also from Aberdeen, arriving by train to Ballater and using every available means of transport to Balmoral.

In 1905 Louise became Princess Royal and the following year she gifted a permanent home for the Braemar Gathering known as the Princess Royal Park. Before that the games had been held at various venues - Invercauld, Braemar Castle, Clunie Park, old Mar Lodge (only once in 1889 marking the marriage of the Duke and Duchess of Fife earlier that year) and on several occasions at Balmoral, the first being in 1887, the year of the Queen's Golden Jubilee.

In 1911, while sailing to Egypt on the liner SS *Delphi,* the Duke of Fife, his wife Princess Louise, the Princess Royal, and their daughters Princess Alexandra and Princess Maud were shipwrecked on 12 December when the ship hit a storm and ran aground off the coast of Morocco. Although the family escaped into a lifeboat, the Duke of Fife caught a chill which developed into pleurisy and he died at Aswan, Egypt in January 1912. His body was brought home by sea in a lead coffin and rested at St George's Chapel Windsor until August 1912 when it was transferred to Mar Lodge. The casket arrived at Aberdeen on Wednesday 7 August and transferred to a special coach attached to the morning train to Ballater. A hearse was waiting to convey the coffin to Mar Lodge. Along the route flags were all flying at half-mast from many of the stately homes as a mark of respect for this notable personality of upper Deeside. The hearse crossed the Victoria bridge and waiting there was a contingent of the Duff Highlanders and by special invitation representatives of the Balmoral Highlanders. The Princess Royal and her sister Princess Maud were waiting at the private chapel of St Ninian and after a short service the casket was lowered into the prepared vault. After the death of her husband, Louise led a reclusive life and in October 1929 at Mar Lodge she was taken ill with a gastric haemorrhage and was brought back to London. She died in January 1931 and was buried in St. George's Chapel, Windsor Castle but later her remains were removed to the chapel at Mar Lodge.

Upon his death, the Duke of Fife peerage, created in 1889, became extinct and was replaced by a peerage created by Queen Victoria in 1900 which allowed the title to pass to his daughters should there not be a son. Hence Princess Alexandra succeeded to the title of 2nd Duchess of Fife. Following the death of her father, the estate was managed by trustees, later passing to Princess Alexandra. In October

1913 she married Prince Arthur of Connaught, her first cousin once removed, a grandson of Queen Victoria. After marriage she was known as Princess Margaret of Connaught, Duchess of Fife. In 1953 Prince Arthur asked that the name of the Braemar Gathering Park be changed to the Princess Royal and Duke of Fife Memorial Park. The Duchess of Fife died in 1959 and was buried alongside her father in St Ninian's chapel at Mar Lodge.

Alexander Ramsay inherited the estate from his aunt but it was sold in 1982 and became a sporting estate with emphasis on creating a skiing development on Beinn a'Bhùird. It was not an unqualified success and in 1989 the estate came under new ownership with the emphasis focused on land management and improvement of facilities. In 1991, while being renovated, the Lodge was extensively damaged by a fire, but was rebuilt and converted into holiday flats retaining many of the features of its days as a hunting lodge.

Mar Lodge Estate became a National Trust for Scotland property in 1995.

Deeside is the Place to Be

The first tourist guide, *A Guide to the Highlands of Deeside,* by James Brown was published in 1831. In his book he was less than generous in his opinion that tourism was beginning to adversely affect the area and was about to be *desolated by cockneys and other horrid reptiles.* Robertson then adds that the air of the Dee Valley *is extremely fresh and pure (as particularly in Durris, Birse and Braemar) by means of its heath and woods; so it is observed that the people along it are very healthy and long-lived. Dr Alexander Fraser of Durris was wont to compare the air there with that of Windsor the finest in England.*

By 1868 when Queen Victoria wrote about her *dear Paradise* in her *Journal of our Life in the Highlands* and told the world about its delights, the tourists had arrived. The railway had opened up the area - the line of the Deeside Railway from Aberdeen reached Banchory in September 1853 and was subsequently extended to Aboyne in

December 1859 and to Ballater in October 1866. Thus, the tourist, intrigued by the royal association, was able to gain entry to the valley from the coast. *Picturesque Deeside begins at Cults,* wrote the Aberdeen Journal in 1886, *nowhere is the Aberdonian craze for building houses, fine houses too - more forcible illustrated.* Thus, Cults and beyond grew rapidly in the early twentieth century thanks to the suburban service which took passengers to town in only 12 minutes. It was not too long before grand houses, including some holiday homes, were built along the whole of the Deeside valley.

Queen Victoria travelled the line twice a year after the death of Prince Albert and much enjoyed the views from the carriage windows. It is even said she ordered that houses built along the railway line should be built the wrong way round so that their front doors faced the train tracks and not the road to avoid her *seeing the resident's laundry flapping in the wind and preferred to have a view of their nicely painted front door*s!

To provide accommodation for people wanting to sample the pleasures of Deeside, some house owners in the summer months would move into smaller accommodation in their gardens leaving the main house for holiday lets. The railway provided the holidaymakers with a very convenient method of travel before the advent of the motor car.

One of the many visitors to Deeside was author Robert Louis Stevenson. When he was on holiday in Braemar in 1881 he complimented the Queen on her choice of Balmoral as her summer residence. In a letter to a friend, he wrote: *The country is delightful, more cannot be said; it is very beautiful, a perfect joy when we get a blink of sun to see it in.* (The weather was bad during his stay). *The Queen knows a thing or two - she has picked out the finest habitable spot in Britain.* Robert Louis Stevenson suffered from a chronic lung condition and prior to coming to Braemar, he had stayed for a month at Kinnaird near Pitlochry for the sake of his health. He later wrote *that while he loved the native air, it did not love him, and the end of this delightful period was a cold, a fly-blister and a migration by Strathardle and Glenshee to Braemar.*

He spent seven weeks in Braemar from 3 August to 23 September. He was accompanied by his father and mother, his wife and her 13 year old son, Lloyd Osbourne. They rented a cottage which had been owned by Miss Mary Macgregor who had died in 1880. It was while on holiday that he wrote *The Sea Cook*. The story grew out of a map painted by young Lloyd Osbourne who suggested to his stepfather that he write a story around it. Stevenson did so, and after dinner each evening, he read what he had written that day. In this way the fascinating tale came into being - on Deeside, far from the scene of the narrative. The cottage where RLS and his family stayed can still be seen in Castleton Terrace just beyond the Scottish Episcopal Church of St Margaret. At the end of the holiday the family would have travelled by train from Ballater to Aberdeen before heading south. Later that year he completed the writing of his book, now named *Treasure Island,* while he was in Davos, Switzerland.

Deeside had become very fashionable as the place for the wealthy to add to their property or build a fine country house with the pleasure of fishing, hunting and of course, to enjoy the rich countryside. In 1869 William Cunliffe Brooks, later Sir William, a wealthy Manchester banker, arrived at Glen Tanar (also spelt Tanner or Tana) as a tenant of Charles Gordon, 11th Marquis of Huntly, who had married his daughter that year. He purchased the estate in 1874 which had been put up for sale to pay for the Gordon family debts. Between the years 1888 and 1899 he acquired large estates on Deeside including Aboyne and Glentanar and he left his indelible mark on the architecture of these estates. A regular visitor to Glen Tanar was the Prince of Wales, later King Edward VII. Another was Lillie Langtry, a socialite of the time, and said to have become the Prince's mistress from 1877 -1880. She would travel to Aboyne by train and in all probability, met the Prince during her visits. Pierre Fouin in his book *Glen Tanar Valley of Echoes and Hidden Treasures* writes *that life for her was dull in a mansion house for a feisty young woman with all the men folk out killing things and boredom had her tobogganing down the main staircase on a silver tray.* Despite her Royal connection, surely she would have not been invited back. Instead, her host ordered his butler to hide away the trays on any future visit! On his death, the estate was bought in 1905 by George Coats of the cotton firm of Paisley who was created 1st

Baron Glentanar in 1916. The house was demolished in 1975 and rebuilt for the Hon Jean Bruce, granddaughter of the first baron.

Another family which set down roots on Deeside were the Keillers of Dundee. In 1886 John Mitchell Keiller and his wife Mary came to Ballater to enjoy the pleasures of Deeside. John was the great-great-grandson of Janet Keiller who along with her husband John had created their version of orange marmalade. Their son James set up the company which in 1797 became James Keiller & Son Ltd. As well as marmalade, it also produced confectionary, preserves and cakes. Their Dundee cake, it is claimed, was a favourite for afternoon tea of Queen Victoria and a century later by the late Queen Elizabeth II. In 1931 the company was awarded royal warrants to supply King George V with marmalade and Queen Mary with chocolate. The company name was retained after successive takeovers until 1996.

In 1886 John Mitchell Keiller bought some 10,000 acres of the Morven and Gairnside estates of Charles Gordon, 11th Marquis of Huntly, whose family had held the lands for centuries. On the estate, at Abergairn, there was a lead mine which Keiller immediately closed as he did not wish industry on his land. The estates had excellent shooting and fishing rights and Queen Victoria had shown interest when the estate was put up for sale but the price of £50,000 was considered too high. Morven hill, on the estate, had been one of the Queen's favourite excursions when she was on holiday at Balmoral. Perhaps she was inspired by George Gordon, later Lord Byron who spent some time during the summers of 1795-97, while staying in Aberdeen and attending the Aberdeen Grammar School, at the farm of Ballaterich on the south Deeside road. Later in life he wrote:

> *When I rov'd a young Highlander o'er the dark heath,*
> *And climb'd thy steep summit, O Morven of snow!*
> *To gaze on the torrent that thunder'd beneath,*
> *Or the mist of the tempest that gather'd below*

Morven Lodge - now demolished (Ian Murray)

The Keillers had come to enjoy holidays in Ballater, originally staying at Morven Lodge, often referred to as the *Shooting Box*. The house was inconvenient for their guests arriving by rail at Ballater. In 1891 they built a more spacious home on the *hill of the oaks* known in Gaelic as Craigendarroch. Rather than building with local granite, red sandstone was used, brought all the way by rail from the Pentland Hills near Edinburgh to Ballater station and then by cart to the site of the new house. John Keiller died in 1899 leaving his son, Alexander, then aged nine, as heir to the family fortune.

Alexander took after his father and enjoyed a life of luxury while on Deeside but he had no interest in the family business and nominated his uncle to be his representative on the board. Instead, his interests were in fast cars and archaeology. He was extremely generous in entertaining his guests and it is said that when he bade farewell to them at Ballater station he would race down to each railway station in turn to be there before the train. Ian Cameron, in an article he wrote for the *Ballater and Crathie Eagle,* suggests *that with four wives in his life time he could have well have been making a last-minute attempt to entreat some lady friend to return to Craigendarroch with him rather than return to the south.*

The house, grounds and fishing were not sold by the Keiller family until 1945 and at the same time much of the land was bought by the Dinnet estate. In 1952 the house became a hotel and later in the 1990s it became the Hilton Craigendarroch. The hotel closed in 2013 and was converted into timeshare suites. The Keiller name lives on as the lounge is called the Keiller Lounge.

The great attraction of Deeside and wide appeal could hardly be better stated than in the words of Captain Blair Oliphant written in 1911: *Here is to be found the best of all that Scotland has to offer to the lover of the beautiful, to the seeker after health and rest, and to the sportsman.*

The Visit of the Shah of Persia to Britain in 1889

Nasser al-Din became Shah of Persia in 1848. In 1842 he was given a camera by Queen Victoria which fascinated the 11-year-old. He loved to take photographs of his childhood as well as keeping a diary of his visits abroad. In 1873 he undertook a tour of Europe and visited London at the invitation of Queen Victoria. He and his entourage, which was vast, stayed at Buckingham Palace from 19 June to 4 July but the Queen remained at Windsor. On their first meeting on 20 June, she invested the Shah as a Knight of the Order of the Garter. He was given this honour on the advice of William Gladstone, the Prime Minister, who was anxious to seek better relations with Persia at a time when there was rivalry in Asia between Russia and the British Raj in India.

His Royal Highness quickly became legend. At one Palace dinner it is claimed the Shah *drank from the spout of the teapot and generally proved himself unfamiliar and disinterested in silverware.* The Palace kitchens prepared a whole sheep nightly for the Shah and his entourage to pick at in his rooms.

When he left such were the stains on some of the carpets that the Queen insisted that Parliament should pay for replacements and that some of the rooms be redecorated.

He was to return to Britain in 1889 but by then the Shah had become much better acquainted with western etiquette. During this visit, which lasted a month, he came to Deeside. On 30 June, Sir Henry Drummond Wolff, the British Ambassador and head of a special British Mission to Persia, made detailed arrangements for the Shah's visit.

Accompanied by Mr Sidney Churchill, British Consul in Persia, he left for Antwerp on 30 June 1889 on board the royal yacht *Victoria and Albert II.* The other royal yacht *Osborne* was also sent over for the Persian Sovereign and his suite. Arriving back in Britain the following day, royal salutes were fired as the yachts passed up the Thames, a route selected to give the Shah the idea of the greatness of London. They were met at Tilbury by the Prince of Wales and his two sons Princes Victor Albert and Prince George of Wales. The Shah disembarked at six o clock at Westminster Stairs and was received by the Duke of Cambridge, a cousin of Queen Victoria and Commander-in-Chief of the Forces, and Prince Christian of Schleswig-Holstein, husband of Princess Helena, Queen Victoria's daughter. The Shah was then escorted to Buckingham Palace where he was to stay while in London. The following day the Shah went to Windsor to be received by the Queen.

The Shah had an extensive tour of England including visiting Birmingham, Sheffield and Liverpool before coming to Scotland by

Nasser al-Din, Shah of Persia
(Royal Collection Trust /
© His Majesty King Charles III 2024)

train. The speed was no doubt carefully regulated. It has been reported that on his first visit to Britain in 1873 he was not happy with the excessive speed of the train that had taken him from Dover to London and had even ordered the immediate execution of the driver! He was hosted at Buchanan Castle on Loch Lomond, the seat of the Duke of Montrose. At a luncheon given in his honour by the Corporation of Glasgow he said: *the beauty of your scenery, the character of your people, the poetry of your country have made the name of Scotland one of the most popular countries of the world.*

On Friday 19 July he reached Ferryhill, the place of exchange of engines from the Caledonian to the Great North. It was the day of the Aberdeen summer holidays and large crowds had gathered to see the Shah. A special platform covered with crimson cloth had been erected opposite where the royal carriage was expected to stop and a guard of honour of the First Volunteer Battalion of the Gordon Highlanders was in place. The train arrived in the specially decorated station just after 4pm and the Shah was welcomed by the Lord Provost and the City Magistrates and was presented with an address before leaving for Ballater. There to greet him at Ballater were Prince Albert Victor, son of the Prince of Wales, and Mr James T Mackenzie of Kintail (later Lord Glenesk).

The Queen had suggested he did not stay at Balmoral, claiming she considered it had a funny smell and had arranged Glenmuick House near Ballater, the country house of James Mackenzie, as a very suitable residence. In 1838 he had gone out to an indigo plantation in India where he made a very substantial fortune. In 1871 he commissioned the building of the House of Glenmuick, overlooking Ballater, completed in 1873. He was a friend of the Prince of Wales, later King Edward VII, who became a regular guest at the house. The house was ideally situated with great stalking opportunities and also excellent grouse moors. One of his many guests who travelled to Ballater was less than complimentary about the house suggesting that its situation *was selected with the view to impress the good people of Ballater rather with the importance of its owner, than to provide a comfortable house for himself and his guests.*

House of Glenmuick
(Royal Collection Trust / © His Majesty King Charles III 2024)

On arrival at Glenmuick, the Shah watched Highland Games on the lawn and then in the evening had dinner with other guests. At the event was Dr Alexander Profeit, who had succeeded Dr Andrew Robertson as the Queen's Royal Commissioner at Balmoral. In a letter to the Queen after the event he wrote that *the whole arrangements were carried out regardless seemingly of expense.*

Later a ball was held in a spacious marquee and for a short time the Shah seemed to take an interest in the Highland dancing but was not over impressed to see men in kilts! Donald Stewart, Queen Victoria's head gamekeeper, was at the ball and he had made arrangements that on the following morning he should take the Shah deer driving in Ballochbuie forest on the Balmoral estate. To ensure a successful stalk on the Saturday, Donald Stewart had two ponies ready, one for his Majesty and the other for his ambassador. The deer had been for some days in the corrie of the Boultshoch on the Balmoral estate.

The Shah was told about the plans for the following day and at once his interest was aroused, as he was a keen sportsman. Through his interpreter, Prince Malcolm Khan, he asked many questions of his host but when it was explained to him that deer stalking required the greatest caution in approaching the deer and required at times crouching down, he lost interest and laughing, said he would never think of going down on his knees. That altered the plans and instead the Shah displayed his skill as a marksman by firing about a dozen shots at a cast iron representation of a deer. In the

Dr Alexander Profeit
(Royal Collection Trust /
© His Majesty King Charles III 2024)

afternoon he and his party, along with Prince Albert Victor and Mr Mackenzie, travelled by coach along the south bank of the Dee to Balmoral Castle where Dr Profeit gave His Majesty a tour of some of the rooms.

While walking in the grounds he saw the statue of John Brown, Queen Victoria's *faithful servant*. He had died in 1883 and at the time the statue stood on a bank beside the Garden Cottage. Initially he was confused and thought it was a statue of the Prince Consort. When it was explained to him Brown's position in the royal household he was lost in astonishment. (When King Edward VII came to the throne in 1901, he ordered that the statue of John Brown be moved to a more secluded place on the estate.)

Statue of John Brown at Balmoral

The royal party then drove to Invercauld House, where for the next two days they were the guests of Sir Algernon Borthwick, MP for Kensington. He was the owner of the *Morning Post* (which merged with *The Daily Telegraph* in 1937). At the time he was renting Invercauld from the Farquharson family - an expensive luxury but one he could afford - the rent alone was over £5,000 a year. The Shah reached Invercauld about 5 pm, and after dinner came more entertainment and another ball.

A HIGHLAND DANCE BEFORE THE SHAH, GIVEN BY SIR ALGERNON BORTHWICK, AT INVERCAULD HOUSE, BRAEMAR

THE SHAH OF PERSIA IN SCOTLAND

Unfortunately, the following day being a Sunday, did not permit the Shah to experience fishing on the Dee. At that time the river was an angler's dream. It was on the upper and lower Invercauld beats that in May 1892 Sir Algernon Borthwick and his son netted 156 fish in sixteen days; on one of the days their combined catch was 25, and on a second 24 were netted and on a third 20 salmon were landed. How things have changed. Sunday, therefore, was a much-needed day of rest for the Shah after what had been a very arduous visit to Britain, allowing him time to indulge in sketching, another of his passions. He left, we are told, with a drawing he had done of a stuffed bird on show in the castle.

On the Monday morning the Shah departed and arrived at Ballater at 11.45, some forty minutes ahead of schedule and before the guard of honour had arrived from their barracks. The Shah and his party boarded the train to await their arrival, but he went out to inspect them before his special train left for Aberdeen. Being the local holiday, large crowds were on Deeside that day which probably, because of the heavy traffic, delayed the train arrival at Ferryhill by 11 minutes instead of the expected time of 1.58 pm. The Lord Provost was there to offer his greetings and he presented His Majesty with a basket of strawberries while the engines were being changed. Before the train left, the Shah, through his interpreter, said to the Lord Provost that *he had greatly enjoyed his visit to Deeside and had much admired the loveliness of the scenery and the beauty of the ladies.*

He was on his way to stay at Hopetoun House, the home of the Earl of Hopetoun (later Lord Linlithgow) who at the time was a Lord-in-Waiting to Queen Victoria. On the following day he was taken to see the engineering brilliance of the almost completed Forth railway bridge, a marvel of Victorian engineering still in use to this day. He then visited Edinburgh and left Scotland for Newcastle. His visit was declared a great success; he had been well entertained and had been shown the best of British technology, which he greatly admired. The Shah's visit to Britain ended on 29 July when he embarked on board *Victoria and Albert II* and sailed round the fleet, then being prepared for a review on 4 August in the presence of Emperor Wilhelm of Germany, Queen Victoria's grandson. No doubt it reminded him of his previous visit in 1873 when he was the guest of honour at the review. He took his leave of the Queen who was at Osborne on the Isle of Wight and then left on the royal yacht for Cherbourg.

Sir Henry Drummond Wolff, who had masterminded the Shah's visit to Britain, wrote: *On this his second visit the Shah gave no evidence of the slight eccentricities that had marked his first journey. During the whole of this tour His Majesty seemed thoroughly to appreciate the warmth with which he was greeted by the crowds.*
When the Shah returned home his secretary communicated with Sir Algernon Borthwick in which he refers to *the pleasantness of his stay and sends a souvenir of his visit in the shape of a ring for Lady Borthwick whose health did not let her take part in the festivities connected with His Majesty's reception.*

The Shah became increasingly unpopular in his home country and seven years later he was assassinated.

The Visit of the Emperor of Russia Tsar Nicholas II in 1896

Note: In the following the spelling Tsar has been used in preference to Czar. Both are acceptable. *Encyclopaedia Britannica* prefers Tsar as does Wikipedia and the Oxford Dictionary.

First it is necessary to establish the link that Britain had with the Emperor of Russia. His bride was Alexandra (known to the family as Alix), the daughter of Princess Alice and granddaughter of Queen Victoria and Prince Albert. But it is interesting to establish how the marriage came about. Alice had married Louis, Grand Duke of Hesse and died from diphtheria in December 1878. Queen Victoria had insisted that the distraught Louis and his four children should come back from Germany to be comforted by her. Alix was only six years old and the youngest but she quickly became Victoria's favourite grandchild. Victoria was determined that she should marry well and even had ambitions of seeing her betrothed to her first cousin, Prince Albert Victor of Wales who was heir to the throne after his father the Prince of Wales, later to become King Edward VII. Alix had already set her heart on marrying Nicholas whom she had first met in 1884 when attending the wedding of her sister Elisabeth to Grand Duke Sergei Alexandrovich in St Petersburg. At this wedding, the 12-year-old Alix met the 16-year-old Grand Duke Nicholas, nephew of the groom and heir-apparent to the Imperial throne of Russia. Queen Victoria did not approve, and in the spring of 1887, she wrote to Alix's sister Elisabeth: *I must tell you that my heart and mind are bent on securing dear Alicky for either Eddie* (the family name for her eldest grandson) *or Georgie. You must prevent further Russians or other people coming to snap her up.*

In 1888 she even arranged a meeting at Balmoral between Prince Albert Victor of Wales and Alix which came to nothing. Instead, the Prince became engaged to Princess Mary of Teck on 3 December 1891 but a month later he died of pneumonia. Sometime later his brother, Prince George, Duke of York (later to become King George V), became engaged to Princess Mary and they were married in July 1893.

Queen Victoria was still opposed to Alix marrying Nicholas and after the betrothal was announced in September 1894 she reflected: *The more I think of sweet Alicky's marriage the more unhappy I am. Not as to the personality for I like Nicholas very much but on account of the country and the awful insecurity to which that poor child will be exposed.*

They were married on 26 November 1894 only weeks after Tsar Alexander's death.

So now to the visit of the Tsar and Tsarina: A newspaper reported on the arrangements that were made at Leith for the arrival of the Imperial yacht in September 1896: *Not only had due honour to be done to the ruler of a mighty empire but provision had to be made for the safety from attacks by political fanatics. The civil and military authorities of this port and the neighbouring capital devoted themselves with assiduity to their duties in this respect. Ample police precautions were taken for thwarting any Anarchist plots, and there was a display of naval and military of the British Crown such as hardly ever before been witnessed so far north in this island. The Channel Fleet which arrived in the Firth of Forth a few days ago. lay at anchor in the Leith roadstead.*

The Imperial Yacht *Standart* anchored off Leith on the morning of Tuesday 22 September. The yacht had been built for Nicholas's father, Emperor Alexander III and was constructed at the Danish shipyard of Burmeister & Wain, but he did not live to see it completed. He died in November 1894; the yacht was launched on 21 March 1895 and had only come into service in September 1896.

Edward, Prince of Wales, and Arthur, Duke of Connaught, two of the Queen's sons, had travelled down to Dalmeny by the royal train some days before and were hosted by the Earl of Roseberry, some distance up the Firth. On the morning of the arrival of the Tsar, they once again joined the royal train which took them to Junction Bridge Station near Leith where they went on board the *Tantallon Castle*, the paddle steamer normally providing a daily service to Forth tippers. We are told *she had been much scrubbed, carpeted and draped to make her fit for royal service.* The greeting between their

Imperial Majesties and their Royal Highnesses *was of the most friendly and, indeed, affectionate character.* After lunch on board all was made ready for the landing at Leith and the journey to Balmoral by the Royal train. While lunch was being served, two Leith tugs were required to bring their 10 tons of luggage ashore.

At 1.30pm the Imperial party left the *Standart* and went on board the *Tantallon Castle*, which immediately cast off and steamed away to the harbour where they were greeted and presentations made by the Provost of Leith and the Lord Provost of Edinburgh. The latter in his welcome said: *We hail your Majesties' visit as an augury that the friendly relations, which exist between the Sovereign and people of the two great Empires under the Russian and British Thrones will not only continue, but be deepened and extended. We earnestly hope that these two peoples, knit together by mutual sympathy will not merely enjoy moral and material prosperity within their own borders, but that their unified influence will be potent in the interests of peace and in advancing the cause of humanity and civilisation throughout the world. We pray that your Majesties may be long spared, and, under Divine guidance and blessing on you rule, may have the joy of seeing your people ever advancing in loyalty, happiness and prosperity.*

It was then time to set off on a carriage procession the mile or so to the Junction Bridge Station. Lining the route from the docks to the station were the Scots Greys, of which the Tsar was an honorary colonel, the King's Own Scottish Borderers and the Argyll and Sutherland Highlanders, all reinforcing the local garrisons of the Enniskillen Dragoons, the Black Watch, and the Royal Artillery.

Notwithstanding heavy rain, the carriages were all open. The Emperor, now cloaked, as were also the Prince of Wales and the Duke, the Prince wearing the Russian uniform of the 25th Kieff Dragoons, and the Duke his Scots Guards uniform. Their Majesties and Royal Highnesses at once entered the Royal train and soon they had left for Edinburgh Waverley Station, and on to the Forth Bridge on their northern journey.

The train made a brief stop at Dundee before arriving at Ferryhill Station, Aberdeen, shortly after 5.30pm. The visit did not meet with universal acclaim and Aberdeen Town Council were initially reluctant to officially welcome the Tsar to the city. However only two days before he arrived, it was agreed that Provost Mearns, attired in official robes and chain of office, should welcome their Imperial Majesties before the train left on its last part of its journey to Balmoral. Later, on reporting on this welcome, the *Bon Accord,* a local weekly paper, commented *when Aberdeen comes to its senses we hope it will be ashamed of the ridiculous part it played over this Tsar business. When the Tsar is at home we do not hesitate to call him a tyrant but, when a man whom they have no sympathy with touches our city on his way to see his grandmother-in-law, the Town Council plays the hypocrite, and fetes he whom they at other times curse.*

A good number of people gathered at Cults and West Cults to welcome the Tsar and Tsarina to Deeside before it got dark. British summer time was not introduced until 1916 and sunset that day was shortly after 6 pm. It had been a day of persistent rain resulting in the decorations, much of it the black and yellow of the imperial colours, becoming somewhat bedraggled. It was reported that *much time and not a little cash had been spent, losing much of their spectacular effect.* Electric light had also been installed, lighting up the station and the square. Their Imperial Majesties reached Ballater about seven o'clock, and were welcomed by the Duke and Duchess of York (later King George V and Queen Mary) before entering their carriages a few minutes later. The rain got even heavier as they set off for Balmoral with a mounted escort of Scots Greys. The Queen left her own apartments and came down to the sitting-room of Princess Beatrice to watch the bonfire on the opposite craig, one of four lit on conspicuous peaks on the Balmoral estate to welcome her guests. A few minutes before 8 o'clock, a mounted messenger arrived to announce the imminent arrival of the Imperial party. There to greet them were the Balmoral men and the Ballater and Crathie Volunteers, bearing lighted torches. The Queen, accompanied by Prince Henry of Battenberg, the husband of Princess Beatrice, welcomed her guests at the door of the castle. The Highlanders raised a rousing cheer, and before the door was finally closed, they marched past in single file. The whole reception was over in a few minutes. The visit was primarily a family reunion with many of the Queen's children and grandchildren travelling specially to Balmoral for the occasion. Nicholas and Alexandra had their ten-month old daughter Olga with them to meet her great-grandmother, Queen Victoria.

The Tsar had a large quantity of luggage and an incident occurred at Ballater station when Charles Davidson, the signalman at the station, was helping load the various pieces into a two-horse brake under the supervisions of one of the Tsar's Cossack attendants. Unfortunately, he put something on that was not wanted and left something off that was, causing the Cossack to argue with him in Russian and threaten him with his stick. A diplomatic incident was avoided when a Russian security guard, who could speak some English, restored peace. Charles later discovered that the Cossack had been demanding that he be flogged!

The Tsar had time to enjoy the pleasures of the estate and on the first day, we are told, he shot a fine stag while on the next it was the turn of the Prince of Wales, later King Edward VII, and his son the Duke of York. It has often been remarked the close resemblance of the

Tsar to the Duke of York. In 1853 the Prince of Wales had married Alexandra, a Danish Princess, whilst in 1866 her sister, Dagmar, had married Tsar Nicholas's father Alexander III - hence the close relationship, as first cousins, of the Tsar and the Duke.

Queen Victoria with Albert Edward, Prince of Wales, Tsar Nicholas II and his family, Balmoral, 1896 September 1896
(Royal Collection Trust / © His Majesty King Charles III 2024)

The stay at the castle was also a time for discussion - Queen Victoria spoke to Nicholas regarding the Eastern Question and her Prime Minister and Foreign Secretary, Lord Salisbury, gained assurances on Russia's intentions towards India.

Members of the British and Russian Royal Families at Balmoral
(Royal Collection Trust / © His Majesty King Charles III 2024)

The Tsar and his wife left Balmoral on the evening of 3 October accompanied by Arthur, Duke of Connaught, and his wife Louise. The Queen wrote in her diary: *At 10 dear Nicky and Alicky left to my regret, as I am fond of them. Went to the door to see our dear visitors leave. There were again the Highlanders bearing torches, but no pipes.*

In a recent book it has been suggested that Balmoral was considered as a possible residence for the Romanovs after they were overthrown by the Bolsheviks in March 1917. King George V was not in favour and withdrew the offer of asylum in Britain. The Tsar and Tsarina were to suffer a terrible death. After months of plotting, they were assassinated late on the night of 17 July 1918 by their Bolshevik captors.

Royal Stations of the Deeside Line

Most of the stations of the Deeside line were of simple construction with few facilities, but three which were used by the royalty and their guests were more ornate and had additional features.

Banchory

Banchory Station c1914

From the opening of the line in 1853 Banchory was the terminus for the royal train until the extension to Aboyne in 1859. There was a refreshment room which was first used by Queen Victoria in 1854 when she alighted from the train on her way to Balmoral. The original station was of simple construction and the concourse was often extremely muddy and had to be hardened by hand.

Because of the royal use of the line, Banchory soon developed into a popular place for visitors and from the opening of the line special excursion trains were popular. In July 1854 it was reported that *56 carriages took 1,700 along the beautiful route of the Deeside line - for the most part to Banchory.* In Alex McConnachie's *Deeside* published in 1900, the author refers to it as *a summer resort for Aberdonians and tourists which takes precedence, for numbers, over all others, while on holidays excursionists visit it literally in thousands. The Hill of Fare protects Banchory from the cold winds of the north and its southern exposure also contributes to its advantages as a health and holiday resort. Unquestionably nature has done a great deal for Banchory; the marvel is that the century had begun* (that is, the nineteenth century) *before the nucleus of a town had been founded in such a delightful situation.*

The station had a turntable and shunting in these early days was done using a horse. Keith Jones, writing for Gordon Walkden's book *About Banchory* records that when *not so employed local shunter William Milne harnessed the horse to a cart to make local deliveries.* There were also workshops to maintain the rolling stock and engines. David Deans, a local man, was the foreman in charge in 1854 but a few years later he was dismissed for misappropriation of funds and emigrated to New Zealand. His job as shop foreman was taken over by his brother Hugh. The railway company were well pleased with his work. Dick Jackson, in his book *Royal Deeside Railway,* records that in 1864 they increased his salary from £110 to £115 plus a free house, fuel and light.

But by the end of the century, a new station was most desperately required. James Coutts, writing in his book *A Dictionary of Deeside* in 1899 called the old station *neither well built nor well situated, being placed at the eastern outskirts close to the churchyard, as if designed for nearness to the dead rather than the living.*

Prior to the reconstruction in 1902, preparatory work was undertaken by building a retaining wall with a right of way path alongside the Dee, known as the platforms but referred to by locals as the *Platties.* The name *platties* comes from the Scot's word *plat* meaning a *flat spot.* Stones were taken in by railway wagons and tipped down the embankment before being craned on to bogies which conveyed them along a temporary track behind the wall where they were lifted into place by a crane. The new station was built further to the west of the original, with wider platforms, extended facilities and a covered foot-bridge and so it served until the closure in 1966.

Aboyne

Originally a two-platform station, with the station building on the eastbound platform, it was considered *commodious and imposing the last word in design.* It served as the terminus of the line until 1866 when the line was extended to Ballater.

Aboyne Station was opened in December 1859 and first used the following August by Queen Victoria at the start of her journey to Balmoral that year. The Huntly Arms Hotel was used as a resting point for the Queen before she left by carriage for the journey to Balmoral. The 10th Marquis of Huntly used to walk down from his home in Aboyne Castle to greet the Queen when she arrived at the station and ensure that all was well for her journey to Balmoral. The 10th Marquis had married Maria Antoinetta Pegus in 1844, five years after the death of his first wife. In 1857 she had cut the first turf for the extension of the railway to Aboyne and as a close neighbour, she had become a friend of the Queen. After the death of the 10th Marquis in 1863, his widow carried out the tradition and was at the station in September 1865 to welcome the Queen on one of the last occasions she used Aboyne on her journey to Balmoral.

Aboyne Station

In 1895-6 a new station was replaced by the GNSR who had acquired ownership of the line. In the *Buildings of Scotland Aberdeenshire South and Aberdeen* it was described as having *a satisfying long front, single-storeyed but with a higher centre for the entrance under a low state roof with carriage canopy in front, anchored at the outer corners by circular towers with baronial cone-roofs with fish scale slating.*

Compared with what James Coutts thought of the original station at Banchory, he was generous in his praise for Aboyne station. In his book *Dictionary of Deeside* published in 1899 he writes: *If first impressions of a place are to be taken from the railway station, Aboyne would come out very favourably the platforms extended and improved so that the station is now the finest on Deeside.*

Ballater

The station was opened on 17 October 1866 by the Aboyne and Braemar Railway, the third of a series of openings by three different companies to connect Ballater with Aberdeen; the others being Aboyne to Banchory by the Deeside Extension Railway and Banchory to Aberdeen by the Deeside Railway.

The original station was far from grand and did not offer the Queen a waiting room. It prompted James Mackenzie of Glenmuick to write in 1884 a private and confidential letter to William Ferguson, Chairman of the GNSR, urging that the station be upgraded and a room be provided for the Queen's use. It would appear that the directors were shamed into action as plans for a new station were drawn up shortly afterwards. Included was to be a royal waiting room modelled on that at Wolferton, the station for Sandringham, the estate in Norfolk which was purchased in 1863 by Queen Victoria for Albert Edward, Prince of Wales, later Edward VII, as a country home for the Prince and Princess.

When Queen Victoria arrived at Ballater on 21 August in 1886 she was able to see the new station and waiting room which met with her approval. It had a plaster strap work ceiling, timber mantelpiece with mirror and decorative stained glass windows. To complete the room there was an adjoining toilet with a floral design bowl.

The architectural guide for Deeside described the station thus - *built in clapboard with deep eaves forming a canopy with decorative bargeboards, also featuring on slender entrance front porte-cochere.* Ten years later it was temporarily painted black and gold, the imperial colours of the Tsar, for his visit to Balmoral.

Outside, in the station square and set into the road, are a series of stones marked the boundary of railway property. Each stone has the letters GNSR carved into it.

Ballater Station had a long curving platform long enough to accommodate the Royal train.

The Final Visits to Balmoral by Queen Victoria

The Queen's love for Balmoral continued to the end of her life, coming twice a year and with the visits becoming extended. Ahead of her Golden Jubilee in 1887, the Queen had specifically requested that her staff should be increased by some representatives from India to help serve at a banquet for heads of state. Karim, the son of a hospital assistant living in the North Indian city of Agra, was one of two servants selected and presented to Victoria as *a gift from India.* Karim joined Victoria four years after the death of her beloved Brown and quickly set to work for the nearly 80-year-old monarch. Victoria wrote that her first impression of the handsome Karim was that he was *tall*

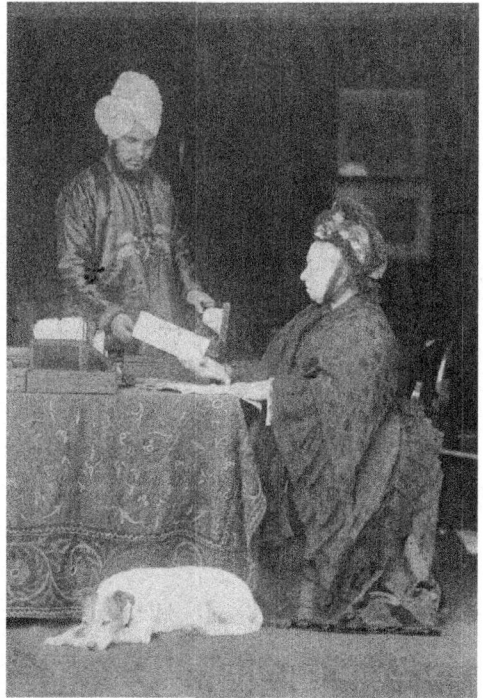

Queen Victoria with Mohammed Abdul Karim (Munshi) 1890
(Royal Collection Trust
© His Majesty King Charles III 2024)

with a fine serious countenance. Victoria wrote in her diary: *I am learning a few words of Hindustani to speak to my servants. It is a great interest to me, for both the language and the people.* She also insisted that Karim should take English lessons so that they were able to communicate directly with each other. Though he was hired as a servant, Victoria quickly promoted him to *Munshi and Indian Clerk to the Queen Empress.* He was given his own accommodation on the royal train and was responsible for serving light meals to the Queen just as John Brown had done in earlier years.

On 19 June 1891 the southbound royal train from Ballater was diverted, so that the Queen could see at close quarters not only the replacement for the Tay Bridge but the recently opened Forth bridge.

Travelling with the Royal train as he had done for many years was George P Neale, the London and North Western Railway superintendent. He was extremely diligent and ensured that nothing should ever go wrong when the Queen was travelling. In May 1894, after a visit to the Manchester Ship Canal, the train was stationary at Carlisle, northbound for Balmoral. It was already after midnight, but Neale was on the draughty platform waiting for the Queen to retire for the night and pass through the connecting bellows from her day to her night carriage. Only then could he give the order for the train to leave. We are told that Neale had taken cold badly and had to relinquish his duties for the rest of the journey. This, no doubt, contributed to the decision that the two carriages be united and the bellows, so hated by the Queen, to be replaced.

On 25 June 1895 G P Neale had made his hundred-and-twelfth and final journey with the Queen; it was time to retire from his royal duties. At Ballater that day, before the departure of the royal train, Prince Henry of Battenburg, husband of Princess Beatrice, asked Neale to join him to meet the Queen. The Queen presented him with a framed engraving of the royal family at the time of her Golden Jubilee in 1887, to thank him for his outstanding service.

ROYAL TRAIN IN 1897
(L & N.W. RAILWAY)

On Saturday 9 November 1895, King Carlos of Portugal paid a private visit to Balmoral. Prince Arthur, Duke of Connaught, greeted the King on his arrival at Aberdeen and ex-Lord Provost of the city, Sir David Stewart, expressed the good wishes of the town's citizens. The King and Prince Arthur joined the train for Ballater where, on arrival, the King was given an enthusiastic welcome. He spent two days at Balmoral during which the Queen invested him as a Knight of the Garter, furthering the good relations that had existed for centuries between Britain and Portugal.

The Queen was probably hoping that in time, one of the daughters of the Duke and Duchess of Connaught might marry into the royal family of Portugal. In 1902 Luis Felipe, the Crown Prince of Portugal, attended the coronation of King Edward VII and met Princess Margaret and Princess Patricia, the daughters of the Duke of Connaught. In January 1905, the Duke and Duchess of Connaught visited Portugal, where they were received by King Carlos and his wife. On that occasion Luis Felipe entertained the young British princesses. The Portuguese hoped that one of the Connaught princesses would become the future Queen of Portugal. But it was not to be. A month later, Princess Margaret fell in love with Crown Prince Gustaf Adolf of Sweden and any thought of marriage of Princess Patricia to Luis Felipe was ended when in 1908 he and King Carlos were assassinated.

In November 1895, Prince Henry persuaded Queen Victoria to allow him to go to West Africa to fight in the Ashanti War. Sadly, he contracted malaria and died in January 1896. Despite her grief, Beatrice remained her mother's faithful companion and was by her side in 1897, the year of the Diamond Jubilee. After the celebrations in London, the Queen was especially pleased to be on her way to rest at Balmoral. The engine of the LNWR train taking the Queen north that year was *Great Britain* (painted red) and from Crewe to Carlisle it was replaced by *Queen Empress* (painted white) and finally from Carlisle to Ferryhill it was drawn by *Jubilee* (painted blue).

On 28 October 1898 Princess Beatrice was once again in Aberdeen to open a bazaar in the Music Hall in aid of the Sick Children's Hospital. The weather was kind and the route was decorated with floral displays at the Joint Station and the Music Hall. She was then entertained to luncheon at the Palace Hotel before returning to Balmoral. The Palace Hotel had been built in 1874 and was taken over by the GNSR in 1891. An advertisement of the time records the many royal guests that patronised the hotel as a rest point for breakfast after an overnight journey from London on their way to visit the Queen at Balmoral.

THE PALACE HOTEL,
ABERDEEN.

Owned and Managed by the Great North of Scotland Railway Co.

EQUIPPED WITH EVERY MODERN ACCOMMODATION FOR COMFORT. LIGHTED BY ELECTRICITY. MECHANICALLY VENTILATED. LIFTS.

EXCELLENT CUISINE.   MODERATE CHARGES.

Hotel Porters attend all Trains.

PERSONALLY PATRONISED by Their Royal Highnesses the PRINCE and PRINCESS OF WALES, The DUKE and DUCHESS OF CORNWALL AND YORK, The DUKE and DUCHESS OF CONNAUGHT, The EMPRESS FREDERICK OF GERMANY, PRINCESS CHRISTIAN and PRINCESS VICTORIA, PRINCESS HENRY OF BATTENBERG, The DUKE and DUCHESS OF ARGYLL, PRINCE and PRINCESS CHARLES OF DENMARK, The EMPRESS EUGENIE, The KING OF PORTUGAL, The KING OF THE BELGIANS, The MARQUIS OF SALISBURY, LORD KITCHENER OF KHARTOUM, and many Distinguished Visitors.

Address MANAGER, Palace Hotel, Aberdeen.

LONDON AND NORTH WESTERN RAILWAY.

ARRANGEMENT OF CARRIAGES

COMPOSING

HER MAJESTY'S TRAIN

From BALLATER to WINDSOR,

On WEDNESDAY, the 20th, and THURSDAY, the 21st JUNE, 1900.

Engine.	Guard.	For Men Servants.	Dressers and Ladies' Maids.	Countess of Antrim. Hon. Mrs. Grant. Hon. Alice Harbord.	Queen's Dresser	Her Majesty and Princess Victoria of Schleswig-Holstein.	Personal Servants	Sir Arthur Bigge. Gen. Cross. Col. A. Davidson. Sir James Reid.	Mr. Muther. Indian Attendance.	For Pages and Upper Servants.	Directors.	Directors.	Footmen.	Guard.
Engine.	Van. No. 210.	Carriage No. 879.	Saloon. No. 73.	Saloon. No. 153.		Royal Saloon.		Saloon. No. 131.	Saloon. No. 71.	Saloon. No. 72.	Saloon. No. 180.	Carriage No. 306.	Truck. No. 100.	Van. No. 272.

‹———— 192 feet 8 inches ————› ‹ Will leave Train at Perth. › ‹———— 306 feet 5 inches ————›

Carriage Plan for Queen Victoria's June 1900 return to Windsor. Accompanying the Queen at the conclusion of her spring visit to Balmoral, was her granddaughter Princess Victoria of Schleswig-Holstein, daughter of Princess Helena.

The Queen's autumn visit to Balmoral in 1900 was to be her last. It had been a particularly difficult year for her. Prince Alfred, Duke of Edinburgh, who had become Duke of Saxe-Coburg and Gotha in 1893, on the death of his paternal uncle, died in July of throat cancer. In October, the Queen received a telegram telling her that Prince Christian Victor, her grandson, had died of enteric fever while serving in the Boer War. He was the son of Princess Helena, daughter of Queen Victoria. The Queen did not have Munshi by her side to offer comfort, In November 1899 he had gone to India to be with his father, who was ill, and did not arrive back to be with the Queen until she had returned from Balmoral in 1900.

On the afternoon of Tuesday 6 November 1900 the Queen, dressed in deep mourning, left Balmoral for the last time. She had requested that no one should be on the platform at Ballater. The weather was *wretchedly gloomy* and with Princess Beatrice (Princess Henry of Battenberg) by her side, she sat at the fire in the royal waiting room and had tea before departure for Windsor.

The *Aberdeen Weekly Journal* carried a full report of the departure: *The Royal saloon occupied the usual position, in the centre of the train, and accompanying Her Majesty was Princess Henry of Battenberg.* In the other saloons were three of Princess Beatrice's family, Princess Victoria, Prince Leopold and Prince Maurice.

The train left promptly at 3.30 and was due to arrive at Ferryhill junction at 4.47. Awaiting its arrival was a large attendance of ladies and gentlemen who had gathered within the enclosure, admission to which was, as usual, by ticket. Respecting the Queen's wishes there was no formal greeting from the Lord Provost, John Fleming, and magistrates of the city. *Punctual to time, the train steamed quietly to the accustomed stopping place. The interior of the saloon was brilliantly lighted, and as the blinds were only partially drawn, Her Majesty could be seen seated near one of the windows. The transference of engines was speedily effected without the slightest noise. Meanwhile a large number of letters and despatches were handed in to the Royal saloon, while the crowd within the enclosure surveyed with interest the operation of filling two large silver tea urns with hot water. This was done on the permanent way near the Royal saloon, presumably in preparation for afternoon tea. After the usual stay of five minutes the train steamed quietly away and was soon lost to sight as it glided round the curve.*

Those present that day would remember that they had been able to pay their final respects to their Queen. She died just over two months later at Osborne, on the Isle of Wight, on 22 January 1901.

More Royal Trains on the Deeside Line

King Edward VII

Queen Victoria died in January 1901 and was succeeded by her son. The visits to Balmoral by the new King and Queen reverted to once a year, always in the autumn. Their first visit was in September 1901 and on arrival at the Joint Station, the King made his way to the Palace Hotel for breakfast, leaving the Queen aboard. The train left for Ballater promptly at 10 am, where they were warmly greeted by the large crowd. The press report noted that *Kodaks were largely in evidence* and as the royal party left for Balmoral *loud cheers renewed again and again.*

In early August 1901 the King and Queen had visited their new yacht *Victoria and Albert III* which had been commissioned in 1899. They used it as their base during the fleet review held at Spithead on 16 August to mark their coronation. Following the review, the royal couple toured the west coast of Scotland and landed at Invergordon on 8 September where the royal train, on this occasion provided by the GNSR, was waiting to take them to Ballater. The King had asked that the visit should be private, and so the welcome was muted.

The coronation of King Edward VII and Queen Alexandra was arranged for 26 June 1902. Unfortunately, some days before the event, the King was diagnosed with acute appendicitis and an operation was performed on 24 June. The coronation was postponed and re-arranged for 9 August that year.

The following year, the King made his way north again on 7 September, travelling on a train from King's Cross provided by the GNSR but *en-route* there was a stop at Ollerton to attend the racing at Doncaster, finally reaching Ballater on 14 September for his customary autumn holiday at Balmoral.

King Edward VII arrives at Ballater Station

Interior of the Royal Saloon 1903

The King and Queen had a very special event to attend in 1906. On 27 September they travelled by the royal train from Ballater to Holburn Street Station, lavishly decorated for the occasion.

Great North of Scotland Railway—Royal Train

The Royal Carriage at Holburn Station, 27/9/06

There they were welcomed to the city by the Lord Provost and the Principal of the University. Leaving from the station in an open carriage, the King and Queen made their way through the decorated streets of Aberdeen to open the extended Marischal College, then part of Aberdeen University and from 2011, the headquarters of Aberdeen City Council. Its ornate granite frontage, which encloses the quadrangle, is the second largest granite building in the world, exceeded only by the Escorial Palace near Madrid.

After the opening of Marischal College, the King and Queen were entertained to lunch in the Town House before making their way to the Joint Station for the journey back to Ballater. The Aberdeen Free Press reported on the following day: *The valley of the Dee was bathed in sunshine yesterday morning. The most distant points in a district, which royalty has made famous and historic, were outlined on one of the most beautiful of autumn days.*

ABERDEEN UNIVERSITY. MARISCHAL COLLEGE EXTENSION.

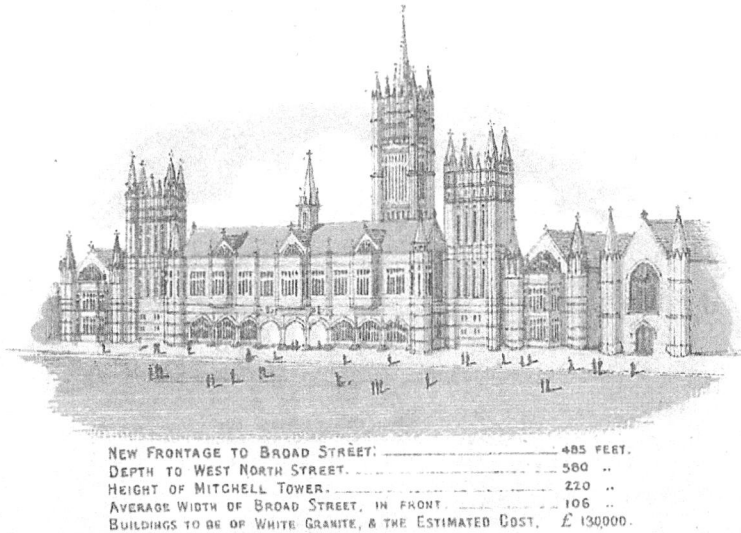

NEW FRONTAGE TO BROAD STREET. _____ 485 FEET.
DEPTH TO WEST NORTH STREET. _____ 580 „
HEIGHT OF MITCHELL TOWER. _____ 220 „
AVERAGE WIDTH OF BROAD STREET, IN FRONT. _____ 106 „
BUILDINGS TO BE OF WHITE GRANITE, & THE ESTIMATED COST, £ 130,000.

In each of the years 1907 to 1910 Queen Alexandra made a journey during her autumn holiday at Balmoral by train from Ballater to Dundee, where she embarked on the royal yacht *Victoria and Albert III* to sail to Denmark. Alexandra's father, King Christian IX of Denmark, had died in 1906 but she made this special visit each year to be with her sister Princess Dagmar, Empress of Russia from 1881 to 1894 and wife of Emperor Alexander III. She was the second daughter of Christian IX of Denmark. After her marriage to Alexander, she was known as Maria Feodorovna. Their eldest son became the last Russian monarch, Tsar Nicholas II. Maria lived for

10 years after the Bolsheviks killed Nicholas and his immediate family in 1918.

Queen Alexandra on her later voyages (1908-10) used the royal yacht *Alexandra* which came into service in June 1908, and was used to transport members of the royal family to European ports.
After the death of King Edward VII in 1910, Queen Alexandra, the Queen Mother, continued to visit Deeside. In 1913 she spent ten days at Mar Lodge, the home of her daughter Princess Louise and was joined by her sister, Princess Dagmar, the Dowager Empress of Russia.

George V

King George V

On Tuesday 9 August 1910, only a few months after accession, King George V and Queen Mary made their first visit to Balmoral. Ballater station had a long, curving platform, large enough to accommodate the royal train, which on that occasion consisted of twelve carriages.

The King was accompanied by two of his sons, the sixteen-year-old Prince Edward, later to be King Edward VIII, and his brother the fourteen-year-old Prince Albert, later King George VI. He was met at the station by the 11th Marquis of Huntly. Before leaving by carriage for Balmoral, the King inspected the guard of honour lined up in the square.

King George V's first visit to Ballater Station

George V had baths installed into each of the 1903 royal saloons made for King Edward VII and Queen Alexandra. Each had a dressing room into which went copper and silver-plated bathtubs, wooden cased and lidded and adequately plumbed for hot and cold water.

1913 was the last year that the King spent time at Balmoral before the outbreak of the Great War. It was not until August 1919 that the King and Queen were once again able to spend some time privately at the castle. The *Aberdeen Free Press* reported that *Deeside was looking at its best with the station lavishly decorated with tasteful drapings of Royal Stewart tartan and an ornamental shield bearing the letters in gold, GR, and a crown in gold cloth.*
The Royal guard was provided by men of the Seaforth Highlanders. The King spent some time acknowledging Corporal Walter Ritchie of the regiment, who had won a Victoria Cross at the battle of the

Somme in 1916. His Majesty had presented him with his VC in November 1916. The VC was introduced in 1856 by Queen Victoria to honour supreme acts of valour during the Crimean War.

On 29 September 1929, Holburn Street Station was used by King George V and Queen Mary when they alighted there on their way to the opening of the extension to the Art Gallery and Cowdray Hall. The return journey to Ballater was made from the Joint Station. The name Holburn Street is named after the *Howburn* over which it passes and has nothing to do with the Holborn of London.

King George V at Ballater Station - August 1930

In 1934, while on holiday at Balmoral, the King and Queen interrupted their holiday to fulfil a very special engagement. It was to launch a new Cunard ship. The story told is that the King was out shooting at Tillypronie, near Tarland,. with Lord Royden, former chairman of Cunard. Royden asked King George V if he would approve the naming of the new ship after *England's greatest Queen*, meaning Queen Victoria, to which the King replied, *My wife would be honoured and delighted.* Hence the ship was named Queen Mary! The story however is not true. The directors of Cunard had already made up their minds that the new ship should be named after HM Queen Mary and Sir Percy, Cunard Chairman, had applied to the Board of Trade to register the name. On 21 July Sir Percy received a letter from an Assistant Private Secretary saying that yard number 534 could be named at her launch on 26 September Queen Mary. The King and Queen travelled from Ballater by royal train to Clydebank for the Queen to name the ship bearing her name. It is not known if Queen Mary was too interested in maritime affairs but on returning to Balmoral after the naming she wrote in her diary - launched a ship today - *pity it rained.*

1935 was to be the last occasion on which the King visited Balmoral. The Royal couple departed Ballater on 27 September and the King died a few months later on 20 January 1936.

Edward VIII

Having succeeded his father King George V in January 1936, King Edward VIII made a customary visit to Balmoral in September of that year. He arrived with his brother the Duke of York on Saturday 19 September. The King and the Duke were both in kilt and plaid of Balmoral tartan. It was to be a short visit as His Majesty was due to leave for London less than two weeks later but not before he had committed a gross error of judgement. He had already informed Edward Watt, Lord Provost of Aberdeen, that he would not be able to open the new Royal Infirmary at Foresthill on Wednesday 23 September as the Court was in mourning. Instead, he sent his brother The Duke of York and The Duchess of York to undertake the opening, while at the same time driving to Aberdeen Station to pick up a guest (later identified as Wallis Simpson). The local paper printed in juxtaposition a photograph of the Duke and Duchess opening the hospital buildings with the headline *His Majesty in Aberdeen - Surprise Visit to Meet Guests.*

On 1 September the King was joined by his brother George, Duke of Kent and his wife the Duchess. There was little pomp for their arrival at Ballater - they had travelled from Aberdeen on a reserved coach attached to the normal Ballater train. The King was to leave from his holiday at Balmoral on Wednesday 1 October and he was accompanied by the Duke and Duchess of Kent. When the train reached Aberdeen, the eight carriages were attached to the London train. It was to be the first and last visit to Deeside as King, before his abdication on 10 December that year.

Edward VIII and his brother the Duke of York - 1936

George VI

After his accession to the throne in December 1936, King George VI, accompanied by members of his family, paid their customary autumn visit in 1937. Arriving by train from London, the journey from Aberdeen to Balmoral was done by road. After a holiday which lasted from Wednesday 4 August to Monday 11 October, the royal train was used for the journey south. In 1938, there was another change of routine. They cruised on the royal yacht *Victoria and Albert III*, arriving in Scotland on 4 August. It was only the second time a reigning monarch had ever arrived in Aberdeen by sea but again, the final part of the journey was done by royal car.

In early September Prime Minister Neville Chamberlain arrived at Balmoral to update the King on Hitler's threat in relation to Czechoslovakia. With the King's approval, Chamberlain flew to Germany to meet Hitler. The King was back in Buckingham Palace by the next morning to be accessible to his ministers at this crucial time. On 21 September, the Queen left the Princesses at Balmoral and joined the King in London, where emergency war measures had begun with the issue and fitting of gas masks. On the 27 September the King and Queen were expected in Glasgow to launch the *Queen Elizabeth*. Because of the intense situation the King could not go, so the Queen returned to Scotland to join the young Princess Elizabeth then aged twelve, and her sister, eight year old Princess Margaret, who had been taken overnight from Balmoral on the royal train to Glasgow to be present at the launch.

It was not until 1 August 1939 that the royal train was used for the journey from Euston to Ballater. On that occasion the train stopped at Drum station for an hour so that breakfast could be served. The Royal Princesses, Elizabeth and Margaret, delighted the crowd that had gathered by coming out onto the platform accompanied by Queen Elizabeth. The visit that year was to be very short because of the outbreak of World War II on 3 September, but before returning to London the King, along with the Queen, was able on 16 September, to make the journey from Ballater to Clydebank to have a secret visit to view the *Queen Elizabeth,* which had been launched the previous year and was still being fitted out on the Clyde. She was too valuable to remain in that vulnerable position, and at the earliest opportunity she sailed for sea trials on 2 March 1940. A deliberate rumour was spread that she would be sailing to Southampton for dry-docking. The Nazis, upon hearing this, planned to have the Luftwaffe bombers waiting. The captain had been given sealed orders to be opened after sailing. Instead of heading for Southampton he was ordered to steam west and the ship arrived safely in New York five days later to join her sister ship *Queen Mary*. The two Queens were among the ships taken over by the government for war service technically known by the acronym STUFT - Ships Taken Up From Trade.

During the war, the King and Queen with the Princesses, paid short visits to Balmoral. It was while they were there in 1942 that they were given the news that Prince George, Duke of Kent, the King's brother, had been killed on 25 August when the RAF Short Sunderland flying boat, in which he was travelling to Iceland, veered off course and crashed into a hillside at Eagle's Rock near Dunbeath in Caithness. The King and Queen returned to London for his funeral on 29 August. During the war, the carriages of the royal train were often *stabled* at Ballater, hidden away in carriage sheds once having been used as garages for the W Alexander & Sons bus company.

King George VI arriving at Ballater Station

Normal visits to Balmoral began again in 1945. In May 1945, after the end of the war in Europe, the King and Queen spent a week at Balmoral. Less than three weeks after the dropping of the two atomic bombs on Hiroshima and Nagasaki, which marked the end of the war in Japan, the royal family once again enjoyed a longer holiday at their highland home. On 25 August 1945 the royal train, as it did in 1939, made a stop at Drum for the royal family to enjoy breakfast and perhaps take the corgis for a walk! At the end of the holiday, King George II of Greece, who had arrived at the castle on 30 September, was with the King as he left Ballater on 4 October. The Queen and the two Princesses spent two more weeks at the castle before returning south on the royal train.

In 1946 the King and Queen welcomed a special guest, General Eisenhower, who was invited to spend the weekend at the castle; it was not however his first visit to Deeside. Eisenhower, as General Supreme Commander of the Allied Expeditionary Force, enjoyed the exclusive use of a train during the period leading to the D-Day landings in Normandy in June 1944. In April 1944 his train took him to Scotland so that he could undertake some military inspections in preparation for D-Day. On his last day in Scotland, the train reached Banchory where, along with General Bedell Smith, his Chief of Staff, they had *respite from their labors by an attempt at salmon fishing as guests of the British liaison officer, Colonel Ivan Cobbold* who had rented Cairnton from the Burnetts of Leys. Cairnton, a short distance from Banchory, has one of the finest beats on the river and the fishing records tell us that on Friday 14 April 1944 Bedell Smith caught two - a 3.4 kg (7½ pound) salmon using a sweep fly and a 3.6 kg (8 pound) salmon using a silver-grey fly on the Grey Mare pool but no mention of Eisenhower. He must have had an unsuccessful day on the river!

On 7 October 1946 the Queen, accompanied by Princess Elizabeth and Princess Margaret, travelled from Ballater to Greenock to watch *Queen Elizabeth* undergoing her sea trials the following day. They went out to join the ship on the Clyde pleasure steamer *Queen Mary II*. The royal party had a full inspection of the ship and the Princesses were given stopwatches to time the measured mile. After this the Queen took the wheel and steered the largest ship in the world down the Firth of Clyde before returning to Balmoral.

Another guest at the castle that summer was Prince Philip, whose father was Prince Andrew of Greece and Denmark, a younger son of King George I of the Hellenes (originally Prince William of Denmark). His mother was Princess Alice, who was the eldest daughter of Prince Louis of Battenburg, who in 1917, had relinquished his German title. King George V created him Louis Mountbatten, Marquess of Milford Haven. Philip was born in Corfu but when he was only eighteen months old, he, along with his family, left Greece when his uncle King Constantine I was forced to abdicate. At first the family settled in Paris but from 1930 Prince Philip had little contact with his father and mother. His father moved to Monte Carlo and his mother, Princess Alice, travelled around Europe before finally returning to Greece. During this time Prince Philip's guardian was Louis Mountbatten.

After being educated in France, Germany and at Gordonstoun in Scotland, Prince Philip joined the Royal Navy in 1939. When at the Naval College, Dartmouth, he had met Princess Elizabeth. During the war the young Princess corresponded with Prince Philip. In the summer of 1946, the King granted Philip permission to marry Elizabeth but the announcement was not to be made public until he following summer after the royal family had returned from their tour in South Africa. When the royal family left Balmoral that year, the King travelled south to Euston on 6 October, followed ten days later by the Queen accompanied by Princess Elizabeth and Princess Margaret.

Princess Elizabeth married Prince Philip in November 1947 but not before the usual holiday was spent that autumn at Balmoral. In 1948 there was time for a spring holiday and again in the autumn. For part of the time the King and Queen were joined by the married couple, now known as the Duke and Duchess of Edinburgh.

The Royal train at Ballater in September 1945 an early visit
by the King after WWII

In 1949 the King and Queen spent a week at Balmoral in early June. On the 5 August, the royal train left from Euston that evening with not only the King and Queen and Princess Elizabeth and Princess Margaret, but also the eight month old Prince Charles on his first visit to Balmoral. Later the Duke of Edinburgh joined the family at the castle.

The King's last visit to Balmoral was in 1951. The King and Queen travelled north by royal train and arrived at Ballater on Friday 3 August accompanied by Prince Charles and Princess Anne. It was during that visit that the King had to travel back to London on the royal train overnight on 7/8 September to have a consultation with his radiologist. A week later he flew to London for treatment and a few days later he was joined by the Queen.

He appeared to be recovering well but on 6 February 1952 the King died at Sandringham. Princess Elizabeth was enjoying a short break in Kenya with Prince Philip and the couple were to stand in for the King on a long-planned tour to Australia and New Zealand. The new Queen had to fly home and arrived back in London the following day to be met by the first of her Prime Ministers, Winston Churchill.

Queen Elizabeth II

Elizabeth's first visit to Balmoral as Queen was during court mourning at the end of May 1952, along with the Duke of Edinburgh, Prince Charles (who after the accession was known as Duke of Rothesay when in Scotland) and Princess Anne. She arrived to spend a quiet week at Balmoral. On Friday 8 August the royal train arrived at Aberdeen Joint Station where the engines were changed before heading for Ballater. The weather was far from kind but it did not deter the Duke inspecting the guard of honour provided by the Black Watch. On 12 September the Queen, a keen racegoer, broke her holiday to travel south to Bawry, near Doncaster, to watch the St Leger. Princess Margaret, who had spent some time on holiday at Balmoral, joined the family for the journey south on 13 October.

Queen Elizabeth II with family at Balmoral - 1953

In 1953, just before the Coronation on 2 June, the family had a short visit to Balmoral but had a much longer holiday in August. This time the weather was kind and in sunshine, the Queen inspected the guard of men of the Argyll and Sutherland Highlanders. The Queen once again interrupted her holiday and went by train to attend the St Leger in September, but this time she was joined by her Prime Minister, Winston Churchill.

Soon after her coronation in June 1953, Churchill had a stroke. On 2 August, at one of his regular meetings with the new Queen, he confided his illness to her and two weeks later she sent an invitation to Churchill, suggesting that he and his wife should join her to watch the St Leger and then travel north with her to spend a few days at Balmoral. Despite the advice of his doctors that such a rail journey might be added strain, he and his wife Clementine travelled to Doncaster on Thursday 11 September, and, after watching the race from the Royal box, joined the Queen on the Royal train to Ballater and by car to Balmoral. He had last been there in September 1928 as Chancellor of the Exchequer, and as Minister in Attendance on King George V he had been invited by the King for four days' grouse and stag shooting. On that occasion he may possibly have travelled to Ballater on the Messenger train.

Royal Train at Ballater 1953

On his visit in 1953 he accompanied the Queen to Crathie Church on Sunday 14 September, having been there with Edward VII forty-five years previously. He and his wife left the castle the following day. The Queen told a friend that *she found the improvement he had made since she had last seen him at the beginning of August astonishing.*

The same pattern continued for several years - short holiday in May and a longer holiday in the autumn. On 5 August 1954 the Queen Mother, Princess Margaret, Prince Charles and Princess Anne came by royal train from Euston to Ballater where they were joined by the Queen who came by air, the Duke of Edinburgh being in Canada.

The late King was already in failing health by the time the designs for the HMY *Britannia* were submitted and just one day before his death, the contract for building was awarded to the John Brown shipyard in Clydebank. The launch by the Queen was in April of 1953 and when it was completed, the royal family used the yacht for cruising around the Western Isles of Scotland. The first time was in August 1955 and it included a stop off at the Castle of Mey, bought by the Queen Mother three years earlier after the death of King George VI. The Queen, the Duke of Edinburgh, Prince Charles, Princess Anne and Princess Margaret all arrived by motor launch to visit the Queen Mother, before reaching Aberdeen on her first visit to the city since her accession. She was welcomed by the Lord Provost, George Stephen, and carried out several engagements in the city before continuing to Balmoral by car.

During the 1959 autumn holiday at Balmoral the Queen was joined for a weekend by President Eisenhower, who had become President in 1953. Now in his second term, he was invited by the Queen to spend the weekend at Balmoral. He had been to the castle in 1946 as guest of King George VI and had met the then Princess Elizabeth. On Friday 28 August 1959, he arrived in Aberdeen by plane from London and was met by the Duke of Edinburgh and driven to Balmoral. Although the Queen was pregnant with Prince Andrew and was not expected to carry out any public engagements, she went to the gates of Balmoral to welcome the President. Eisenhower shook the Queen's hand warmly, with the remark *How nice of you to let me come.* The Queen had also met the President in 1957 when she visited Washington. He was the first of many US Presidents that the late Queen met. Seemingly, during the President's visit in August 1959, President Eisenhower fell in love with the Queen's drop scones which she had prepared at the family barbecue. In his book, *Waging Peace*, President Eisenhower wrote:

One quality of the royal family that has always intrigued me is the informality which prevails when its members are at home among themselves, particularly at Balmoral. At the afternoon picnic by the lake, the Queen acted as hostess and simple housewife, gracefully cooking the dropped scones over a charcoal burner for her eight or ten guests. I tried to help as a waiter; I am quite sure that I was adjudged by her Majesty as somewhat less than competent in this department. In any event, after tasting dropped scones for the first time I asked the Queen for the recipe and she later sent it to me.

The Royal train continued to be used by various members of the royal family, but not on such a regular basis, though the tradition of inspecting the royal guard in the forecourt of Ballater station continued right up to 1964. On 12 August that year, the Queen arrived to perform that duty accompanied by Prince Charles, Princess Anne, Prince Andrew and Prince Edward. At the beginning of September the Queen travelled south with Prince Charles and Princess Anne for the start of the new school year, leaving the two younger Princes at Balmoral. The Queen came north again to Glasgow on 3 September to carry out engagements with the Duke in Glasgow. The following day the royal train took them to Dalmeny, where the Queen officially opened what was then Europe's longest suspension bridge across the Firth of Forth at Queensferry. The new bridge sits beside the old cantilever rail bridge, opened in 1890 by the, then Prince of Wales. Afterwards, the Queen and Duke drove across the bridge in the royal car and returned across the Forth by ferry, marking one of the final crossings of a service which had lasted for almost 800 years. They then joined the train for the journey back to Ballater.

The last royal train left from Ballater on the evening of Thursday 14 October 1965. The Queen was travelling alone on her way to Dalmally for the opening the following day of the Cruachan Dam. After the ceremony the Queen left from Taynuilt for Alyth Junction where she was joined by the Duke of Edinburgh at Glamis Castle as guests of Fergus Bowes-Lyon, nephew of Queen Elizabeth the Queen Mother and a first cousin of the late Queen. The Queen and the Duke then rejoined the royal train on 18 October for the journey to Euston.

The Beeching Report, published in 1963, was the death sentence for the Deeside line and despite many local petitions, the passenger service was withdrawn on 28 February 1966. For many years the Royal yacht *Britannia* was used to cruise the islands off the west coast of Scotland, docking in Aberdeen for the start of the royal family's autumn holiday. Departure from Balmoral was by road to Aberdeen to join the train to London. It was in August 1997 that the late Queen arrived in Aberdeen for the last time aboard *Britannia,* decommissioned later that year. The Granite City had always had a particular affection for *Britannia* and the ship's complement regarded Aberdeen as their Scottish home-from-home. Aberdeen had seen *Britannia* more frequently than any other port, apart from Portsmouth. In 1998 the vessel was decommissioned and is now berthed at Leith where it is open to the public as a tourist attraction.

The Royal family now travel by air to Aberdeen, or some other northeast airport, then onward by road to Balmoral.

Memories of the Royal Deeside Line

The last passenger train left on a round trip to Ballater on Saturday 26 February 1966, but goods traffic continued for a few more months with the final train leaving from Culter on 30 December that year. After 113 years the line was finally closed but the rails were not lifted for another four years. The former line is now a popular walkway. What is now known as The Deeside Way is used by walkers and cyclists with many sections suitable for horses. The route follows the line of the old Royal Deeside railway from Aberdeen, starting at the Duthie Park as far as Banchory. It then passes through woodland and farmland by way of Scolty and Potarch to Kincardine O'Neil and Aboyne before rejoining the old Deeside line to Ballater.

Ferryhill was the terminus of the Aberdeen Railway and it was from there that the first timetabled train left on Thursday 8 September 1853 bound for Banchory. Up until 1920, Royal trains seldom entered the Joint Station, preferring to use Ferryhill Junction for exchanging engines. The Ferryhill Railway Heritage Trust was set up in 2007 to take over the remaining buildings and turntable with the aim to restore it and transform the site into a working railway heritage site for the north-east of Scotland. The turntable, originally constructed in 1906, was repaired in Kintore before being lifted back into place in December 2019. Ferryhill Railway Heritage Trust chairman, Dr Jon Tyler, told BBC Scotland: *It's fantastic to see the turntable back in position after 18 months of repairs. We will have the facility to accept charter steam trains in Aberdeen for the first time for 40 years.*

The success of the Trust in restoring the turntable was recognised at a 2019 event held in London and a plaque was unveiled in July 2021, delayed because of covid restrictions.

The turntable was used in July 2023 by the iconic *Flying Scotsman,* heading an excursion train, visiting Aberdeen before returning to Edinburgh.

The turntable at the site of the former railway station.

In 2024 the work on the restoration of the Caledonian engine shed, the office building and the water tower was fully completed.

The Caledonian engine shed at Ferryhill Junction.

Many of the stations have disappeared altogether, but some have survived and are now private houses while others have been converted and used as business premises.

The three royal stations have all suffered in different ways. At Banchory the station was completely demolished in 1970 and a housing estate now fills the space. The old retaining wall built in 1902 remains and the only surviving buildings are the engine sheds which were first used as a council store. Between 1994 and 2024 they have been used by Roy Cowie, a landscape services company, which has two royal warrants. The sheds displayed the coat of arms of her late Majesty the Queen and the badge of Charles, Duke of Rothesay, as Prince of Wales, now King Charles III. Following the Queen's death in September 2022, all warrants granted by the late Queen became void and companies awarded a warrant by the then Prince of Wales may be allowed to use the King's insignia if it is reissued. Another small reminder of the line is a fountain opposite the entrance to the library in Scott Skinner Square. A granite plaque with the background showing the old railway station in Banchory was unveiled by Miss Lesley Grant in December 2006. The inscription reads:

This drinking fountain was originally from Banchory Railway Station, part of the Old Deeside Line. It was rescued when the line closed in 1966 and was donated by former Provost Jean J. Grant when the Square was built in 1993.

To keep the Deeside line alive, the Royal Deeside Railway Preservation Society was formed in 1996 with the aim of restoring a section of the line from Milton of Crathes to Banchory, a total distance of just over 3.2 km. In 2012 the former Victorian station building at Oldmeldrum was moved to Milton and reconstructed. It now houses a shop, ticket office and waiting room. Along a restored track, the Society operates diesel engines and two steam locomotives *Bon Accord*, built for the Aberdeen Corporation Gasworks in 1897; and *Salmon* built in 1942, and named after HMS *Salmon*, a British submarine, which in December 1939 sighted the German liner

SS *Bremen*. The commander of the *Salmon* decided not to torpedo the liner because he believed she was not a legal target. His decision not to fire on *Bremen* possibly delayed the start of unrestricted submarine warfare in the war.

An electric railcar, known locally as the *Sputnik,* was introduced in 1958 on the Deeside line. It was powered by batteries which were recharged at Aberdeen and Ballater. In 1962 problems were being experienced with the railcar and it was withdrawn, but much later in 1984, it was restored to working order and used for some time on the privately-owned East Lancashire Railway, north of Manchester. In 2001 the Society gained ownership of the railcar but it took another five years before it returned to the track. It may be a forlorn hope that one day the railcar will be able, under its own powe,r to operate again on this section of the old Deeside line.

In August 2015, after hearing that vandals had smashed windows on a 1965 railway carriage, the then Duke of Rothesay made a donation through his charitable foundation. On 17 April 2017 the then Duke paid a visit to Milton where not only was he able to fulfil every boy's dream of driving an engine, but he also unveiled a plaque on a coach named *Birkhall*.

King Charles III at Milton of Crathes Station

Another royal visitor to the restored Deeside Line was the late King George Tupou V of Tonga on 10 January 2008 on his way to visit the Duke of Rothesay at Birkhall.

2008 King George Tupou V Tonga at Milton of Crathes Station

The Society has extended the line via the Birkenbaud level crossing to a new station, Riverside Halt. The group has ambitious plans to extend the line nearer Banchory. A new Deeside Way bridge across the Burn of Bennie was lifted into place on the 15 December 2020 to allow the Deeside Railway to use the original railway bridge.

After the 1966 closure of the original Deeside line, Aboyne station was abandoned for many years until the, then council-owned building, was converted into several shop units with a new housing development to the rear. The frontage was well restored retaining its many fine features bringing it back to its former glory.

A plaque at the west end of the frontage of the building records the history of the station.

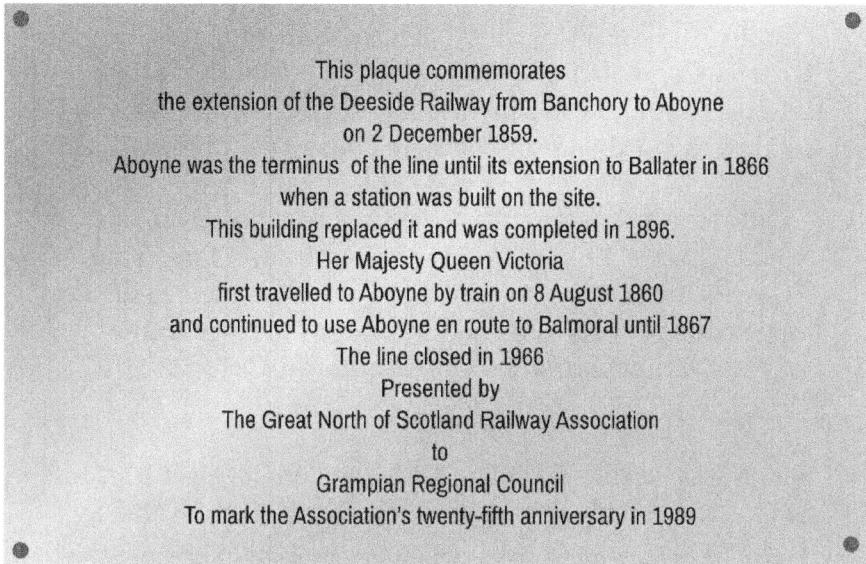

> This plaque commemorates
> the extension of the Deeside Railway from Banchory to Aboyne
> on 2 December 1859.
> Aboyne was the terminus of the line until its extension to Ballater in 1866
> when a station was built on the site.
> This building replaced it and was completed in 1896.
> Her Majesty Queen Victoria
> first travelled to Aboyne by train on 8 August 1860
> and continued to use Aboyne en route to Balmoral until 1867
> The line closed in 1966
> Presented by
> The Great North of Scotland Railway Association
> to
> Grampian Regional Council
> To mark the Association's twenty-fifth anniversary in 1989

In December 2015, a steering group was formed to consider transforming this historic station into a centre for the village community. Included among the suggestions were *turning the site into a cafe, arts centre, community radio station or space for local charities and volunteers*. Although Aberdeenshire Council expressed a willingness to work with the local community to develop the ideas, no progress has been made and it remains an unfulfilled project.

Ballater Station fell into disuse after the closure but it was refurbished and used first as a local area office by Kincardine & Deeside District Council. In 1986, the centenary of the opening of the royal waiting room, the Great North of Scotland Railway Association suggested that when the Queen was on her way to Balmoral she should make a stop at the station. On 16 August her car arrived where she was greeted by the Lord Lieutenant of Aberdeenshire, Sir Maitland Mackie, before being invited to inspect the royal guard, which that year was drawn from the 1st Battalion the Black Watch.

A plaque was unveiled marking the event. It read:

> **This Plaque was presented by the Great North of Scotland Railway Association to the Kincardine and Deeside District Council commemorating the rebuilding of the Ballater Station in 1886, when the Royal Waiting Room behind this wall was opened for Queen Victoria's use,**
>
> **Ballater Station for over a century was the scene of Royal arrivals and departures through six reigns from Queen Victoria to Queen Elizabeth. Many heads of government, and other public figures arrived at the Station on their way to Balmoral Castle**

The station was needing to be upgraded, and on 20 April 2001, after a £1 million revamp, the then Prince Charles, Duke of Rothesay, performed the formal opening. The upgraded station now housed shops, a restaurant, visitor information and a Victorian themed display of the arrival of Queen Victoria at the station; and to complete the attraction, the Queen's waiting room was set out recalling the day in 1900 that she left from Deeside for the last time. The formal handover to mark the completion of the £247,000 improvement project to the station square took place on 16 September 2002 and it included the unveiling of the old Great North of Scotland Railway boundary marker stones on the roadway which had been uncovered during excavation work.

Later the Prince suggested that a replica carriage would enhance the display of Queen Victoria's arrival at the station. His wish was granted when on 30 January 2005, a 15-tonne replica of his great-great-great-grandmother's day coach of 1869 was set in place on the old platform. The handcrafted carriage was copied from an original on show in the National Railway Museum in York. The £450,000 project was funded by the European Regional Development Fund, Scottish Enterprise Grampian, VisitScotland, the Heritage Lottery Fund, Aberdeenshire Council and First Group.

The Duke of Rothesay had been kept informed on progress and along with the Duchess of Rothesay, he formally unveiled the carriage on 9 April 2008, the day of their third wedding anniversary. At the ceremony he said: *I am thrilled that at last this project has come to fruition because it was seven years ago that I came to open the restored station which had looked quite sad for a long time. I have incredible special memories of arriving and departing from there as a child. It is wonderful to see it brought back to life.*

THE
ROYAL VICTORIAN CARRIAGE
OPENED BY
THE DUKE AND DUCHESS OF ROTHESAY
9TH APRIL 2008

Interior of the Royal carriage at Ballater Station (Jim Henderson)

In the early hours of 12 May 2015, a disastrous fire destroyed most of the station, though the royal carriage was saved. Plans were put in place to replace this iconic station, and phoenix-like it rose from the ashes in a £3 million restoration project which brought it back into use as a tourist centre, library and bistro. The old royal waiting room, which had been completely rebuilt, is now a private dining room. Later, the award-winning Rothesay Rooms which had started life in 2015 as a pop-up in the village, moved to the station. The Prince's Foundation, which operated the catering at the station, hosted a preview evening at the Carriage (the name given to the bistro restaurant) on Friday 19 August 2018 and on the following Monday it opened to the public. In November 2022 the Prince's Foundation handed over the catering to a new company but retained the lease.

The five diamond-shaped flagstones (mentioned on page 107), inscribed GNSR, have once again been set into the new road layout on the station square as a reminder of former days.

Restored waiting room at Ballater station 2024

The exterior was rebuilt to look identical to how it was before the fire. One noticeable change was replacing the red-painted wooden features of the old with a green paint in a shade known as eau-de-nil, the colour used in the early days of the railway.

In December 2019 the station was given a coveted railway heritage award by the judges who described it as a *jewel in the crown and an astonishing display of craftsmanship.* The award ceremony was held in London and it drew personal comments from HRH The Princess Royal, the guest of honour at the event, as Ballater was well known to her. The plaque was not unveiled until July 2021 because of covid restrictions.

Postscript

Queen Victoria first visited Deeside and Balmoral, her *Dear Paradise*, in 1848 and continued to do so for the next fifty-two years. When she left for the last time in November 1900 she was to return to Windsor and then to Osborne on the Isle of Wight, where she died two months later.

As a toddler, our late Queen was at Balmoral in September 1928. Winston Churchill, later to become her first Prime Minister, was a guest of King George V and during his visit he wrote to his wife: *There is no one here at all except the Family, the Household &*

Princess Elizabeth aged 2. This last is a character. She has an air of authority & reflectiveness astonishing in an infant.

Along with her sister Princes Margaret she was to enjoy many holidays at Birkhall with her father and mother, then the Duke and Duchess of York, and later at Balmoral when her father became King in 1936. Her love for Balmoral continued when she became Queen in 1952. It was widely thought to be her favourite residence and it was there that she died on 8 September 2022. The community of Ballater, less than eight miles from Balmoral, considered the Queen to be more of a friendly neighbour than a monarch. King Charles III came to Birkhall along with the Queen Consort, Camilla, on the day after the funeral to mourn their loss. As Prince Charles, he had first visited Birkhall in August 1949 when only eight months old. In later life the house he inherited after the Queen Mother's death in 2001 was described by him *as a unique haven of cosiness and character.* In October 2022 he was back in Ballater and on Tuesday 10 October, in the Victoria and Albert Halls, he thanked the local community for their support as the late Queen's cortege had made its journey down through Deeside to Aberdeen and then south, first to Edinburgh and later by air to London.

The King has already shown his continuing love for Deeside. We can be assured that he will carry on the tradition of spending time on Deeside, a place which, in so many ways, means so much to him.

Note: At the Coronation of King Charles III, on 6 May 2023, Camilla was crowned Queen Camilla.

Appendix 1

Royal children of Queen Victoria and Prince Albert

Queen Victoria and Prince Albert were the first royals to use the Deeside line. The use of the royal train continued with successive monarchs and their families until the closure of the Deeside line in 1966.

Princess Victoria, Princess Royal 1840. She married Friedrich Wilhelm of Prussia in 1858. Friedrich became the emperor of Germany in March 1888 but died in June 1888, just 99 days later. She died in 1901.

Prince Albert Edward, Prince of Wales 1841. He married Princess Alexandra of Denmark in 1863. He succeeded Queen Victoria as King Edward VII from 1901 until his death in 1910. Queen Alexandra died in 1925.

Princess Alice 1843. She married Prince Louis of Hesse in 1862 becoming Grand Duchess of Hesse. She died in 1878. Prince Louis died in 1892.

Prince Alfred 1844. In 1874 he became Duke of Edinburgh and in 1874 he married the Grand Duchess Marie, daughter of Tsar Alexander II of Russia. He became Duke of Saxe-Coburg and Gotha in 1893 on the death of his paternal uncle Ernest II. He died in 1900 and his wife in 1920.

Princess Helena 1846. In 1866, she married Prince Frederick Christian of Schleswig-Holstein. He died in 1917 and she reverted to Princess Helena until her death in 1923.

Princess Louise 1848. In 1871 she married John Douglas Sutherland Campbell, Marquis of Lorne, later the Duke of Argyll. She became Marchioness of Lorne upon marriage in 1871 then Duchess of Argyll from 1900 until her death in 1939. Her husband died in 1914.

Prince Arthur 1850. In 1874. he became Duke of Connaught and Strathearn and in the same year he married Princess Louise Margarete of Prussia who died in 1939. He died in 1942.

Prince Leopold 1853. In 1881 on his marriage to Princess Helena Frederica of Waldeck he became Duke of Albany. He died in 1884 and his wife in 1922.

Princess Beatrice 1857. In 1885 she married Prince Henry of Battenberg who died in 1896. In 1917 she reverted to Princess Beatrice until her death in 1944.

Royal children of King Edward VII and Queen Alexandra

Prince Albert Victor of Wales 1864. In 1890 he became Duke of Clarence and Avondale until his death in 1892.

Prince George of Wales 1865. In 1892 he became Duke of York and from 1901 Prince of Wales then King George V from 1910 until his death in 1936. He married Princess Mary of Teck in 1893 who died in 1952

Princess Louise of Wales 1867. In 1889 she married Alexander 6th Earl of Fife who on marriage became 1st Duke of Fife. He died in 1912. Princess Louise became Princess Royal in 1905 until her death in 1931.

Princess Victoria of Wales 1868. She never married and from 1910 was known as Princess Victoria until her death in 1935.

Princess Maud of Wales 1869. In 1896 she married Prince Carl of Denmark. In 1905 she became Queen of Norway as the wife of King Haakon VII who died in 1957. She died in 1938.

Prince John of Wales died shortly after his birth in 1871.

Royal children of King George V and Queen Mary

Prince Edward of York 1894. In 1901 he became Prince Edward of Wales and from 1910 Prince of Wales until becoming King Edward VIII in 1936. He abdicated in December 1936. He married Wallis Simpson in 1937 and until his death in 1972 was known as Duke of Windsor. His wife the Duchess of Windsor died in 1986.

Prince Albert of York 1895. In 1901 he became Prince Albert of Wales. In 1920 he became Duke of York. He married Lady Elizabeth Bowes-Lyon in 1923. He became King George VI in 1936. until his death in 1952. Queen Elizabeth, the Queen Mother, died in 2002.

Princess Mary of York 1897. In 1901 she became Princess Mary of Wales and from 1910 Princess Mary. In 1922 she married Viscount Lascelles who on the death of his father in 1929 became 6th Earl of Harewood. In 1932 Princess Mary became Princess Royal until her death in 1965. Her husband had died in 1947.

Prince Henry of York 1900. In 1901 he became Prince Henry of Wales and from 1910, Prince Henry. In 1926 he became Duke of Gloucester until his death in 1974. In 1936 he married Lady Alice Christabel, daughter of the 7th Duke of Buccleuch. The Duchess died in 2004.

Prince George of Wales 1902. From 1910 Prince George. In 1934 he became Duke of Kent. In 1934 he married Princess Marina of Greece and Denmark. He was killed in an air accident in 1942, and the Duchess of Kent died in 1968.

Prince John of Wales 1905. From 1910, Prince John until his death in 1919.

Royal children of King George VI and Queen Elizabeth.

Princess Elizabeth 1926. She married Prince Philip of Greece and Denmark in 1947 who was given the title Duke of Edinburgh by the King. Princess Elizabeth became Queen in 1952. Prince Philip died in 2021 and the Queen in 2022.

Princess Margaret 1930. She married Anthony Armstrong-Jones in 1960, created Earl of Snowdon by the Queen. Princess Margaret died in 2002 and her husband in 2017.

The children of Her Late Majesty Queen Elizabeth and Prince Philip:

Prince Charles	1948
Princess Anne	1950
Prince Andrew	1960
Prince Edward	1964

All travelled on the royal train to and from Ballater before the line was closed in 1966, as did the family of Princess Margaret and Antony Amstrong-Jones:

David Armstrong-Jones	1961
Lady Sarah Armstrong-Jones	1964

Appendix 2 – Royal Family Tree

Queen Elizabeth and Duke of Edinburgh Great-Great-Grandchildren of Queen Victoria

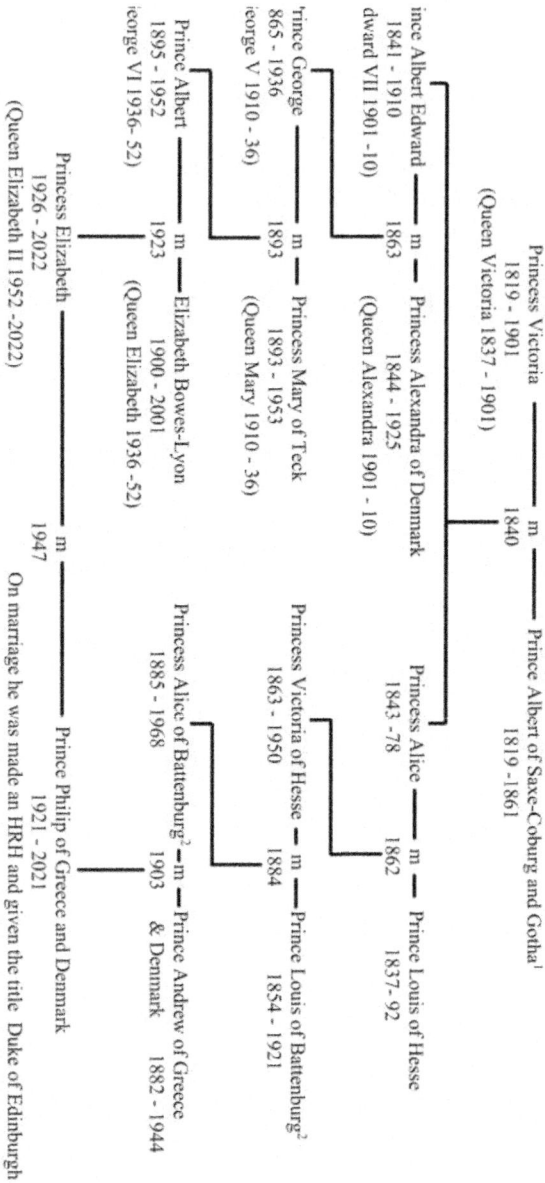

Princess Victoria 1819 - 1901 — m 1840 — Prince Albert of Saxe-Coburg and Gotha[1] 1819 -1861
(Queen Victoria 1837 - 1901)

ince Albert Edward 1841 - 1910 dward VII 1901 -10) — m 1863 — Princess Alexandra of Denmark 1844 - 1925 (Queen Alexandra 1901 - 10)

Princess Alice 1843 -78 — m 1862 — Prince Louis of Hesse 1837- 92

'rince George 865 - 1936 eorge V 1910 - 36) — m 1893 — Princess Mary of Teck 1893 - 1953 (Queen Mary 1910 - 36)

Princess Victoria of Hesse 1863 - 1950 — m 1884 — Prince Louis of Battenburg[2] 1854 - 1921

Prince Albert 1895 - 1952 eorge VI 1936 - 52) — m 1923 — Elizabeth Bowes-Lyon 1900 - 2001 (Queen Elizabeth 1936 -52)

Princess Alice of Battenburg[2] 1885 - 1968 — m 1903 — Prince Andrew of Greece & Denmark 1882 - 1944

Princess Elizabeth 1926 - 2022 (Queen Elizabeth II 1952 -2022) — m 1947 — Prince Philip of Greece and Denmark 1921 - 2021

On marriage he was made an HRH and given the title Duke of Edinburgh

[1] In 1917, the name of the British royal house Saxe-Coburg and Gotha was changed to Windsor because of anti-German sentiment

[2] In 1917 the Family Name of Battenburg was changed to Mountbatten because of anti-German sentiment

Mountbatten–Windsor is the personal surname used by some of the male-line descendants of Queen Elizabeth II and Prince Philip, Duke of Edinburgh. Under a declaration made in Privy Council in 1960, the name Mountbatten-Windsor applies to male-line descendants of Queen Elizabeth II without royal styles and titles.

Appendix 3
Royal Yachts

Since the time of Queen Victoria, the Royal family has had the following Royal Yachts which have been used not only for ceremonial purposes but for short voyages and cruises by the Royal family.

Royal George (1817 - 1842)

Victoria and Albert (1843-1855)
remained in service as *Osborne* (1855-1867)

Victoria and Albert 2 (1855-1900)

Osborne (1870-1908)

Victoria and Albert 3 (1901-1937)

Alexandra (1908-1925)

Britannia (1954-1997)

Further Reading

Many books have been written about the Deeside Railway. The author found the following of particular interest and recommends them to those who wish to explore the Old Deeside Line in more detail. They are listed in chronological order of the original publication date.

A History of the GNSR, Sir M Barclay-Harvey   Published 1940
The Great North of Scotland Railway, H A Vallance,   Published 1965
The Royal Deeside Line, A D Farr   Published 1968
Stories of Royal Deeside's Railway, A D Farr   Published 1971
The Royal Trains, C Hamilton Ellis   Published 1971
The GNSR Album, A E Glen, I A Glen and A G Dunbar   Published 1980
Royal Trains, Patrick Kingston   Published 1985
The Deeside Line, Dick Jackson   Published 1994
Royal Deeside's Railway, Dick Jackson   Published 1999
The GNSR- A New History, David Ross   Published 2015
The Deeside Line, W Stewart Wilson   Published 2016
The Deeside Line - Scotland's Royal Railway, Keith Fenwick   Published 2023

For an account of the campaign to save the Deeside Line see:
Scotland's Lost Branch Lines, David Spaven   Published 2022.

The Deeside line stations as they were and with the same view today:
Then and Now on the Great North Volume 1,
Graham Maxton and Mike Cooper   Published 2018,

Guides for those who wish to walk the old line as it is today:
The Deeside Way, Peter Evans   Published 2021
The Deeside Way A Companion Guide, Kelly Morrison   Published 2023

Acknowledgements

Several people and organisations have kindly offered their assistance and resources during the writing of this book. These include:

Gordon Casely
Great North of Scotland Railway Association
Banchory Heritage Society

Photo Credits

For most part, old prints and postcards have been used to populate the text with visual content. Where this has not been possible, images have been used under Creative Commons License or with specific consent. We are very grateful to these organisations and individuals for their permission.

The Royal Collection Trust
Jim Henderson
Ewen Rennie
Ian Murray

The Authors

Stewart Wilson, retired Rector of Banchory Academy, is the life-long recorder of events, people and the history of Deeside.
He has produced a history of Cunard Line illustrated in stamps and old postcards part of which is on view in the libraries of the Cunard ships.
Stewart has given a lifetime of service to the Scout Movement and has been a Rotarian for over 40 years.
His other interests include the preservation of the historic huts of the early explorers of Antarctica, maps of Kincardineshire and Robert Burns.

Chris Engel is a retired oil industry geologist and former local business owner. He was founding secretary and then chairman of the Grampian Transport Museum. For the last seven years Chris has been lead voluntary mentor on the successful Greenpower STEM project at Banchory Academy.
He has been a member of Banchory Rotary for over 20 years. His interests include local history, genealogy, gold prospecting, metal detecting and travel adventure.

Royalty and the Deeside Railway is the second collaboration between Stewart and Chris.

We welcome comments and corrections.
royalty@crathes.com

Printed in Great Britain
by Amazon